# THE BIG BOOK
## OF
# SMALL EQUINES

# THE BIG BOOK
# OF
# SMALL EQUINES

## A Celebration of Miniature Horses and Shetland Ponies

JOHNNY ROBB and JAN WESTMARK

Skyhorse Publishing

Skyhorse Publishing books may be purchased in bulk at special discounts for sales promotion, corporate gifts, fund-raising, or educational purposes. Special editions can also be created to specifications. For details, contact the Special Sales Department, Skyhorse Publishing, 307 West 36th Street, 11th Floor, New York, NY 10018 or info@skyhorsepublishing.com.

Skyhorse® and Skyhorse Publishing® are registered trademarks of Skyhorse Publishing, Inc.®, a Delaware corporation.

Visit our website at www.skyhorsepublishing.com.

10 9 8 7 6 5 4 3 2

Library of Congress Cataloging-in-Publication Data is available on file.

Print ISBN: 978-1-63220-514-8

Printed in China

*This book is dedicated to small equines everywhere, whose soft noses and clever personalities spread joy and goodwill wherever they go. Long may you run, my little friends.*

# Contents

# Introduction

*Tami Hoag*

Every rider has a story, and nearly all of those stories begin with a pony. My story is no different. I was born into a non-horse family, but as soon as I could put sentences together, I started in with, "Can I please get a pony?" My parents steadfastly clung to the belief that I would outgrow this desire as my older siblings had outgrown tap dancing and wanting to play the saxophone. No such luck. When one Christmas they gave me a grooming box with a curry comb and brush in it (thinking this would somehow placate me), my first remark was, "When is the pony coming?"

Eventually, my relentlessness paid off, and my first pony, Smoky, came into my life, and my life was never the same again. With Smoky I learned tenacity, as he was young, barely broke to ride, and bucked me off every chance he got. I kept getting back on, proving to my parents that I was not going to give up on my goal of becoming a horsewoman. Smoky went back to the pony farm for a more advanced rider, and Dan, the pinto Shetland Pony, came to teach me joy and confidence.

Dan was the quintessential family pony, with an enormous character and a heart of solid gold. He packed me everywhere, usually bareback, and often times wearing a fedora—the pony, not me. He was the perfect babysitter, the dream pony every horse-crazy kid imagines. Dan and I were inseparable. We dressed up in costumes and went in local parades. He pulled a cart full of neighborhood kids to the A&W, where his reward was a vanilla ice cream cone. My father—who by now was completely infected with the horse bug—taught Dan to climb the brick steps to the front porch of our house. My very first horse show was with Dan. I drove him in a homemade cart with wheels salvaged from a Model A car. We placed fifth out of five, but I got a big pink ribbon and never looked back.

I now ride and compete at the highest level of my sport of dressage. My mounts are taller at the shoulder than I am and graceful beyond imagining. But they owe a debt of gratitude to their much smaller cousins for helping to shape me into the rider I am today. Ponies taught me responsibility, compassion, and sportsmanship. Ponies provided the opportunity for family togetherness and the basis for building friendships. Ponies were my partners, my companions, my confidants. I remember them all fondly and with a warm heart.

# THE BIG BOOK
## OF
# SMALL EQUINES

# Shetland Ponies and Miniature Horses: Outstanding Equines That Truly Fit In

**W**elcome to the wonderful world of the small equine. Shetland Ponies and Miniature Horses have woven themselves into the fabric of American life. What makes these tiny equines so endearing and so enduring? Some might say it is their tenacious natures packaged in such small, yet dynamic bodies. Few who have had the pleasure of getting to know a Shetland Pony or Miniature Horse will deny that their spirit is enormous in comparison to their size.

Wynn Norman, breeder of the immortal Theodore O'Connor, credits Shetland Ponies' longevity to their keen powers of observation. "Without being both visually observant and sensitive to their environment, they never would have survived," says Wynn. She goes on to say they are smart and that it takes an intelligent trainer to keep them engaged and bring out their best.

Miniature Horses were said to be coveted and collected by ancient royalty. Those who could have anything desired to possess these tiny horses and equated them to the finest jewels and treasures of their era.

Spirited, smart, and sought-after are qualities that still describe today's Shetland Ponies and Miniature Horses, a century after they were first known to have been imported to the United States. They have reared their tiny heads in our culture: in literature and film, of course, as well as the still popular "ponytail" hairdo and Hasbro's "My Little Pony" toy craze of the 1980s and the subsequent *My Little Pony* movie and television series.

From John Steinbeck's *The Red Pony* to Walter Farley's *Little Black, a Pony,* we have read about them, dreamed about them, and enjoyed them. Including childhood pony rides and circus ponies and parades, Americans have never been shy about expressing their fascination with small equines. And the love affair shows no signs of waning.

Today, as land resources dwindle and our high-speed world sometimes leaves us wishing for a simpler era, small equines make more sense than ever. They fit into our environment and can help improve our quality of life. And perhaps it is just this, their ability to both *fit in* and *stand out,* that makes our small equines so endearing and, indeed, so enduring.

# A Brief History of Our Small Equine in America

America has a crystal-clear love affair with small equines, a love affair that started as soon as Shetland Ponies and Miniature Horses arrived in the United States. There are endless colorful stories about how the adorable small equines made their way to America—almost as many as the coat colors the small and captivating equines have.

## History of the Shetland Pony

History shows us that Shetland Ponies originated in the desolate Shetland Islands north of Scotland and are one of the oldest breeds. Due to the harsh living conditions of the island, the Shetland Ponies remained small, rarely growing taller than forty-two inches at the withers. Their short, compact bodies and long, thick manes and tails combined with their hardy, dense coats allowed Shetland Ponies to survive and thrive on very little food and shelter.

The Shetland's small size proved valuable in the European coalmines, and in the mid-1800s Shetlands were shipped to Europe, where they became a valuable commodity. A British mine owner, the Marquis of Londonderry, kept

PHOTO BY Aurora Boyington

track of the pedigrees of the Shetlands and, along with other mine owners, started the first British pony registry. The first British Shetland Pony Stud Book was printed in 1891.

Two men were instrumental in bringing the first Shetlands to America, helping to start an explosion of small equines in our country. Robert Lilburn of Emerald Grove Farm in Janesville, Wisconsin, was the first to import a herd of Shetlands from the Marquis of Londonderry in 1884. Lilburn quickly became the owner of the largest herd of Shetlands in America, and many of today's ponies trace their ancestry to Lilburn's herds.

Another early importer of Shetlands was Eli Elliott from West Liberty, Iowa. He imported three different shipments of Shetlands. All of the ponies came over on ships—one shipment alone brought almost 150 ponies. Elliott was also instrumental in establishing the government of the American Shetland Stud Book, which started in 1889.

Countless Shetland Pony owners will forever be grateful to the men who imported the first soft and fuzzy ponies to America. It seems that as soon as the Shetland's four tiny hooves touched American soil, the ponies were embraced with a genuine love that continues to this day.

## History of the Miniature Horse

While the Miniature Horse is one of the fastest growing breeds in the United States, their history is a little fuzzier than the Shetlands. A common misconception is that the Miniature Horse was bred down from full-size horses, but most historians argue that point. In fact, when the first American Miniature Horse Registry Stud Book was established in 1972, many of the founding Miniatures were recorded as being sired by registered Shetland Ponies.

◄ Feeding time at a Miniature Horse farm.

◄ Small equines were often used as "workhorses" before they became popular as pets and show animals.

PHOTO COURTESY OF the ASPC/AMHR and its members

PHOTO COURTESY OF the ASPC/AMHR and its members

Several myths surround the development of the Miniature Horse, including the theory that their small size was a result of being trapped in a canyon for many generations. Other reports state that Miniature Horses were bred as pets for European royalty, but historical research hasn't been able to validate either of these theories.

What we do know about Miniature Horses in the United States is that two different men were influential in introducing them to our country: Smith McCoy of West Virginia and Moorman Field of Virginia. Since the arrival of the tiny and colorful equines—much like the Shetland Pony—the Miniature Horse has woven its way into the fabric of America.

In the early 1900s, Smith McCoy bred small ponies in West Virginia, and the pint-size equines used in the coal mines were referred to as "pit ponies." When the coal mines turned to automation, McCoy found that the smaller he bred his Miniature Horses, the more of a novelty they became. His herd quickly rose to around a hundred Miniature Horses, and people came from far and wide to see and purchase the diminutive equines.

Moorman Field also bred, raised, and supplied Miniature Horses to the Virginia coal mines, and he and McCoy became friends as a result of their pony dealings. Field became quite successful as a Miniature Horse breeder, a career that lasted over fifty years. Most scholars believe that many of today's Miniature Horses can trace their ancestry back to Field's "midget ponies," as he called them. During the 1960s, it was said that Field's herd of Miniature Horses became so large that they numbered over five hundred head.

The future of the Miniature Horse no longer lies in the darkness of the bleak coal mines but instead rests in the hands of Miniature Horse enthusiasts who breed, raise, and show the small wonders. Miniature Horses also make wonderful pets, a fact that thousands of Miniature Horse owners across the country can attest to.

≺ People have always found it easy to transport and care for Shetland Ponies and Miniature Horses.

# A Bit About
# the Small Equine Breeds

One factor that has influenced the versatility and popularity of Shetland Ponies and Miniature Horses in the United States is the fact that the registry recognizes several types of small equines that are suitable for a variety of equestrian pursuits. While committed to maintaining the very best qualities of the breeds' origins, the registry has listened to needs of the small equine enthusiasts, enabling these small equines to be as useful and popular today as they were when they first came to the United States over a century ago.

# AMERICA'S SHETLAND PONIES

The American Shetland Pony Club recognizes three distinct types of Shetland Ponies: the Classic Shetland Pony, the Foundation Shetland Pony, and the Modern Shetland Pony. In addition, the organization has registries for two types of Shetland crosses: the American Show Pony and the National Show Pony. The goal of the registry is to have a Shetland Pony suited to almost everyone's needs.

All the small equines in the American Shetland Pony Club share the best attributes of the original Shetland Ponies imported from the Shetland Isles over 120 years ago. Americans fell in love with Shetland Ponies the minute they arrived, and that love affair continues today. The American Shetland Pony Club

⅋ A youth driver competes his pony.

PHOTO BY Washburn Photography

PHOTO BY Barbara Bower

⋏ A Miniature Horse plays peek-a-boo.

was formed to preserve the bloodlines of the Shetland Pony and to improve and refine the breed. The result is the versatile Shetland Pony we know in America today.

All the recognized Shetland Pony types and crosses share the prominent Shetland Pony qualities. American Shetland Ponies come in almost every color: black, bay, chestnut, gray, palomino, buckskin, and various pinto color patterns. There are also signature Shetland colorings, such as silver dapple and chocolate dapple coats, that literally change color from winter to spring. The only coloring that is not accepted in the Shetland Pony registry is Appaloosa.

Along with offering an array of coat color choices, Shetland Ponies are athletic, quick learners, and extremely hardy. They generally have excellent hooves

ᐱ Pan's Atomic Particle takes his young rider to the winner's circle.

and a propensity toward soundness and good health. These qualities, combined with their versatility and endearing dispositions, have contributed to their ongoing popularity over the past 120 years.

## The Classic Shetland Pony

Classic Shetland Ponies are refined versions of their Scottish ancestors. They have been selectively bred for a hundred years, and the result is a sturdy pony with appealing conformation. Classic Shetlands can be up to forty-six inches at the withers. They are the perfect-sized starter pony for children. From their early history of pulling ore carts in coal mines, Shetlands have retained an innate driving ability, and their popularity as a driving pony for children and adults alike is ever growing. Classic Shetlands can be found driving along country lanes or holding their own in competitive driving events.

The versatile Classic Shetland Pony can be found in almost every equine role: from children's leadline and short-stirrup competitions, to school ponies, to driving teams with four or more ponies in hand. Whatever the challenge, the ever-appealing Classic Shetland Pony is ready to excel.

While these ponies are hardy, they require the same health care as their larger cousins, although their feed and stabling requirements are in proportionately smaller amounts. Owning a Classic Shetland does not require expensive equipment; equipment can range from the barest essentials, such as simple grooming tools, a halter, bridle, and saddle, to the harness equipment necessary for a hitch of multiple ponies or the elegance of an antique carriage.

Classic American Shetland Ponies are said to raise the spirits of everyone they come in contact with. They have been used successfully in therapeutic programs for the physically and mentally challenged. While they are an ideal starter pony for children, they are also an excellent choice for adults for driving, showing, and simply enjoying. The Classic American Shetland has an appeal that lasts beyond childhood and is one of the main reasons that the American Shetland Pony remains so popular decade after decade.

## A Pony—and a Buddy—of Her Own

Like most horse-crazy little girls, Mary Phelps always dreamed of having a pony of her own. It didn't seem like much of an option growing up in a non-horse family, but Mary never gave up hope. "Every birthday I would blow out my candles and wish for a pony," she said.

Now in her fifties, Mary's dream has finally become a reality. "I finally got my wish," Mary said, adding that it makes her feel like a little girl again.

△ Mary Phelps and her Classic American Shetland Pony Master's Bonnie Buddy.

PHOTO BY *Phelps Photography*

"I have a Classic American Shetland Pony named Master's Bonnie Buddy, and he is to-die-for cute!"

Mary, a photographer and owner of the dressage Web site DressageDaily .com, said she bought Buddy on an impulse but hasn't regretted a moment of the year they have spent together. "I missed having horse breath on my face,"

⌃ A Classic Shetland demonstrates the art of showing.

Mary said. "I had property in Kentucky, and I kept visualizing driving on it, as I had driven on and off my whole life."

After Mary bought Buddy, she started taking driving lessons, and that's when she discovered a whole new world. "I have taken Buddy on a lot of pleasure weekends for recreational carriage drivers. There is a great deal of opportunity to travel to beautiful properties where they have wonderful events for people who are passionate about driving."

PHOTO BY Alicia Slocumb

⋏ Jet's Coed Princess, a Classic Shetland Pony, was the 1999 and 2000 Reserve National Champion Classic Mare.

PHOTO BY Jodie French

◄ The beauty of a Classic Shetland Pony.

Buddy and Mary have also spent the last year competing, and Mary is thrilled with their success. "One thing that is great about the sport of driving is that the women get to dress up—you get to wear a hat and a nice scarf and feel pretty," Mary said. "You can also take your dog along. When we were in Florida we competed in the Florida Carriage Classic Driving Show, and we won the Carriage Dog class with Buddy and my dog Tasha, a miniature Welsh Corgi."

While Mary is living out her childhood dreams with the adorable Buddy, she is also finding out how much she truly enjoys the pony world. "One of the things I really love about Buddy is his personality. Ponies have a unique personality—they are almost like a dog," she said. "People are always surprised

Woodmere's Dancin' In The Dark, a Classic Shetland Pony, sired by J.T.'s Sprinkles On Top.

PHOTO BY Alicia Slocumb

to learn he is a Shetland Pony. They are expecting a Thelwell-looking pony, but Buddy is fancy and has a tremendous heart." Indeed, one might truly say that Buddy is a Classic!

## The Foundation Shetland Pony

PHOTO BY Alicia Slocumb

⋏ Alicia Slocumb of Woodmere Shetlands shows off her handsome Foundation Shetland Masters Delightful Dude.

Foundation Shetland Ponies most closely resemble the original Shetland Ponies imported from the Shetland Islands. While they are more refined then their imported ancestors, Foundation Shetlands are smaller and more conservative in type. Standing no taller than forty-two inches at the withers and exhibiting more bone and substance, the Foundation Shetland Pony truly represents the foundation that all the American Shetland Ponies originated from.

Foundation Shetland Ponies are shown in as natural a state as possible. While they are shown clipped, clean, and neatly turned out, any artificial applications are prohibited. Foundation Shetland Ponies are versatile and useful ponies, and breeders and owners take special pride in their bloodlines and breed characteristics, which are the most closely linked to the original Shetlands imported from the Shetland Islands.

PHOTO BY Alicia Slocumb

◄ J.T.'s Sprinkles On Top and Alicia Slocumb at the 2002 Shetland Pony Congress, winning the Classic Open Country Pleasure Driving Championship.

PHOTO BY Alicia Slocumb

J.T.'s ➤
Sprinkles On Top
at the beach.

## Sprinkles On Top: A Foundation Pony with a Little Something Extra

"As J.T.'s Sprinkles On Top's name suggests, he is a pony with a little something extra," says owner Alicia Slocumb. Alicia and her mom, Bonnie Taylor, purchased four Shetland ponies to cross with Arabians, but their plan never materialized. They fell so in love with the ponies that they began dispersing their Arabians; Woodmere Arabians became Woodmere Shetlands.

The one pony that really "drove" Alicia and her mom to move to the Shetlands was a Foundation-bred gray, J.T.'s Sprinkles On Top. He led Alicia to become active in the formation of special recognition and registration papers for Foundation-bred Shetland Ponies within the ASPC. Sprinkles had the size,

PHOTO BY  Barbara Johnson

↖ Splish splash, a small equine enjoys a bath.

correct conformation, pretty head, and level topline that are the trademarks of a Foundation Shetland Show Ponies.

Shown in both halter and driving, Sprinkles became one of the all-time most successful Foundation Shetland Show Ponies. After winning several National Championship titles, Alicia and Sprinkles ventured out to take on the big leagues in CDE driving.

The mighty mane of a ➤ Miniature Horse blows in the breeze.

PHOTO BY Barbara Bower

Graham's Supreme ➤ King, a Classic Shetland Pony owned by Tom Graham, shows off his spunk in the field.

PHOTO BY Cathy Franks

Their record-setting ways continued with wins at the Live Oak CDE, one of the most prestigious CDE driving events held in the United States. After the win, Sprinkles even began receiving fan mail!

"Sprinkles On Top is the best horse I have ever had the pleasure of owning. He is the 'one' horse you might ever find in your lifetime," says Alicia. Today Sprinkles enjoys his well-deserved retirement at Woodmere Shetlands, although he occasionally comes out to make an appearance at major events, and he still receives fan mail.

⅄ Buckeye WCF Miss Ohio, a Modern Shetland Pony filly.

PHOTO BY PanGraf Productions

⋏ A Modern Shetland rocks the ring in liberty.

# The Modern Shetland Pony

Modern Shetland Ponies combine the beauty and hardiness of the Classic Shetland with the excitement and animation of a Hackney pony. The result is truly elegance in motion. This sophisticated pony with its extreme action and

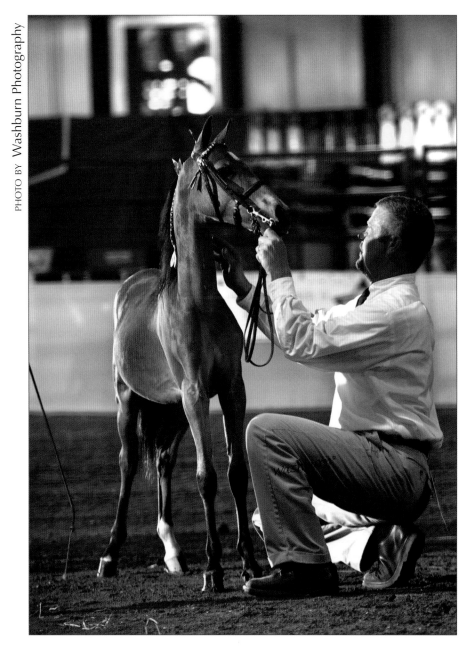

PHOTO BY Washburn Photography

◁ Showing off for the judge in Modern Halter.

spirited personality is truly at home in the show ring. Modern Shetland Ponies are shown in two height categories, under forty-three inches at the withers and between forty-three and forty-six inches at the withers. They excel in performance classes, including roadster, fine harness, and pleasure driving.

A well-trained Modern Shetland makes an athletic, responsive mount for a child and can be used for everything from gymkhana to the popular pony jumper division. A good headset, superb carriage, and high action most often define a great Modern Shetland performance pony. This is an elegant animal, with all the pomp and sophistication of a carriage horse and the hardiness of a pony. Modern Shetlands are a thrill to watch and even more exciting to own and compete. They are often a favorite of converted owners from the Saddlebred, Arabian, Morgan, and Hackney breeds.

⋎ Trot on!

PHOTO BY Washburn Photography

*Washburn©*

## A Modern Shetland Pony That Dazzled the Show World

Winning a World or National Championship Show is the goal of many small equine owners, but capturing the title year after year is almost too much to hope for. Thanks to the dazzling star quality of a Modern Shetland Pony named Hollywood Dazzle, the Brumm family of Indiana watched their little gelding win championship after championship—turning the pony's show life into a Hollywood movie waiting to happen.

Hollywood Dazzle, who is now in his twenties and happily living out his retirement in his pasture, was inducted into the Hall of Fame as a ten-time National and nine-time World Champion for Formal Pleasure Driving. "He was gorgeous in the show ring, and he really had great show presence. He truly is one out of a million, and we have been blessed to have such a great animal," said Garry Brumm, of AG Stables, whose parents Gus and Mary Brumm own the championship pony. "Hollywood also had multiple wins as National Champion Modern Pleasure Gelding in Halter. I don't think he was ever beaten in that division."

Garry grew up on a Shetland Pony farm, so it was only natural that his four children would fall in love with the breed. "We bought Hollywood Dazzle as a two-year-old from Barb Heywood," Garry recalls. "My daughter Keaton won the championship with him five times in a row, then I took over the reins for four years, followed by my son for a year."

While Hollywood Dazzle was famous in the American Shetland Pony show world, his fame also extended into the rest of the equestrian world. "He was the only Shetland Pony to ever grace the cover of the USEF's *Equestrian Magazine*," Brumm said, referring to the April 2002 issue. "The story was on Shetland Ponies, and Hollywood was on the cover and featured in the story."

◅ A Modern Shetland Stallion knows how to show off in the ring.

During Hollywood Dazzle's Hall of Fame ceremony, the entire Brumm family gathered to thank the pony whose star had shone for so long. "He had been shown by all of us and was so much fun to handle," Garry said.

While the Brumm family is still active in the Modern Shetland Pony world—breeding, raising, and showing ponies—they will never forget the remarkable pony that spent so many years dazzling everyone he met.

## The American Show Pony

PHOTO BY Washburn Photography

Drivers of ➤ all ages can enjoy an American Show Pony.

◄ Showing an American Show Pony in style.

PHOTO BY Washburn Photography

With their animated gait and brilliance, the American Show Ponies are similar to Modern Shetland Ponies. However, American Show Ponies can measure up to forty-eight inches at the withers. They can be of Shetland or Hackney lineage or a combination of the two. The American Show Pony Registry was established to accommodate larger ponies that did meet the Modern Shetland requirements, as well as provide a show division for a segment of show ponies that was unserved. These larger, flashy ponies are especially suited to driving and draw a lot of attention in the show ring.

The American Shetland Pony Club offers national and world championship-level competitions for American Show Ponies and recognizes their unique accomplishments with special year-end awards for top ponies in the division.

⋏ A precious Modern Shetland foal.

⋏ Stepping out in the ring.

Action, ➢
action, action in
the show ring!

## The National Show Pony

The newest small equine recognized by the American Shetland Pony Club is the National Show Pony. National Show ponies are required to have one purebred Shetland or Miniature parent and can measure up to a full 14.2 hands at the withers. National Show Pony divisions for hunters, Western, and driving are currently being integrated into Shetland Pony shows. These larger National Show Ponies will enable children to enjoy riding a pony with Shetland attributes for longer. In addition, they will serve adults as a larger carriage pony for a variety of uses.

⋏ National Show Ponies can be driven or ridden.

## America's Gold Medal Shetland Cross Pony: Theodore O'Connor

There is no better example of the value of incorporating Shetland bloodlines and characteristics than the great Theodore O'Connor, owned by Olympians Karen and David O'Connor. Theodore O'Connor—known as Teddy to his fans—was truly the "people's pony." The fact that he was one-eighth Shetland Pony was a heritage that Teddy carried proudly. His dam, Chelsea's Melody, was 13.0 hands, half-Thoroughbred, one quarter Arabian, and one quarter Shetland Pony, and Teddy grew to be a 14.1¾ Sport Pony that caught the attention of the entire nation.

Teddy, along with his Olympic rider Karen O'Connor, made history in 2007 when Teddy became the first pony to compete at the prestigious Rolex Three-Day Event. Karen and Teddy thrilled the crowds, who turned out in record number to see the super pony competing against the world's biggest and best horses. Teddy and Karen didn't disappoint their fans—the small but mighty Teddy finished third overall and won the "Best Conditioned Horse" award.

PHOTO COURTESY OF THE Oaks of Lake City

⋏ Olympian Karen O'Connor riding the late Teddy O'Connor.

⋏ National Show Ponies can measure up to 14.2 hands.

Teddy's fairytale life included being named the 2007 USEF Horse of the Year, although many of his Shetland fans shook their heads and grinned at his title. They were well aware that he should have been called "Pony of the Year."

Teddy went on to make gold-medal history when he and Karen represented the United States in the 2007 Pan American Games in Brazil. The duo helped

Small but mighty, a small equine shows he can act like a big horse. ➢

PHOTO BY  Bob Langrish

the team win a gold medal, and Teddy also became "the little pony that could" when he and Karen won the individual gold medal.

Teddy's fan base grew, and Karen often said that she had never known a horse to have such an impact on an industry. Expectations were high—and his fans were on cloud nine—when Teddy and Karen were short-listed for the 2008 Hong Kong Olympic Games. Sadly, Teddy suffered a fatal accident at home in Virginia before his Olympic dreams were ever realized, and he was euthanized on May 28, 2008.

The very impressive part-Shetland Pony is missed by countless fans, who believe in their hearts that Teddy would have gone on to even more amazing

PHOTO BY Stuart Vesty

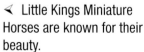

◄ Little Kings Miniature Horses are known for their beauty.

A picture-perfect ➤ meeting of Miniature Horses.

PHOTO BY Johnny Johnston

victories. And while Teddy's one-eighth Shetland heritage would not have qualified him for the National Show Pony registry, he was a great ambassador for the Shetland breed and the value of Shetland bloodlines in performance ponies.

## The American Miniature Horse

One of the most popular and beloved of all the small equines is the American Miniature Horse. Whenever Miniature Horses go to shows, fairs, schools, or

PHOTO BY Johnny Johnston

⅄ Lucky Four Imperial Intrigue, a 33" American Miniature Horse.

other institutions, they are people magnets. The ever-increasing popularity of American Miniature horses is a testimony to their endearing dispositions, versatility, and practicality. The American Miniature Horse Registry is the original registry for the Miniature Horse and recognizes two Miniature Horse size divisions. Division "A" Miniatures are up to thirty-four inches in height, and Division "B" Miniatures are between thirty-four and thirty-eight inches tall. Like Shetlands, Miniature Horses come in a full spectrum of coat colors. Unlike Shetlands, spotted Appaloosa coloring is an accepted and popular coloring in the American Miniature Horse Registry. Miniature Horses have become increasingly popular with both children and adults. These versatile little horses can do just about everything a full-sized horse can do. They are big fun in a small package.

Today's Miniature Horses are bred for superb conformation and outstanding dispositions. The result is a beautifully proportionate little horse that is suitable

PHOTO BY Johnny Johnston

Miniature Horses ➤ have become very popular, thanks to their endearing personalities.

to a variety of uses. Miniature Horses also require similar care to that of a full-sized horse, but, based on their size, they require much less space. Dwindling land resources have also contributed to the Miniature Horse's growing popularity. Miniature Horses are also rarely shod. They are shown without

PHOTO BY Washburn Photography

▲ A Miniature stallion competes.

Little Kings ➢
Psyched Up Buck

PHOTO BY Stuart Vesty

shoes and require only regular trimming to keep their hooves in good form. Miniature therapy horses, however, often wear "mini-sneakers" to keep them from slipping on linoleum or wood floods when they visit hospitals, nursing homes, and schools.

ʌ Miniature Horses are well-suited for the show ring.

Miniature Horse shows are hosted around the country and attract large numbers of Miniature Horse owners of all ages. The Miniature National Championship Show hosted each September in Tulsa, Oklahoma, is one of the largest all-breed horse shows in the United States. Miniature Horse shows offer a variety of classes from halter and showmanship to obstacle driving and the speedy roadster driving—and everything in between. Miniatures are well-suited for everyone, from the novice horse person to the consummate show professional. Miniature Horses are extremely versatile. Their roles vary from backyard pet to gorgeous show horses to therapy horses for persons with special needs and companions to the elderly. Whatever your interest in horses, it is likely there is a Miniature Horse suitable for the job!

Shetland and ➤ Miniature owners love to photograph their small equines on the beach.

PHOTO BY Alicia Slocumb

## Lola, the Picture-perfect Mini

Lola, a Miniature Horse that stands only twenty-four inches tall, is a petite package. She has become a seasoned professional when it comes to having her photo taken and making public appearances. According to her owner Sandy, the tiny wonder came into the world with a "Here I am!" attitude and was named Lola because she was so "Lowla to the ground."

⋏ Lola loves the camera, and dressing up is part of her fun.

➤ Lola shows off her book *The Wonderful Life of Lola: A Day at the Beach.*

PHOTO COURTESY OF ASPC/AMHR and its members

"Lola is a little person in a Miniature Horse body," Sandy said. "She stared life at only sixteen inches tall and wore extra-small dog-size blankets for months."

Lola made her nursing home debut at only seven months of age and hasn't slowed down since. Now seven years old, the adorable bay Mini with the long, flowing mane and tail lives the life of a debutante. When not visiting nursing homes, church groups, clinics, hospitals, or schools, Lola can be found riding the carousel at amusement parks, hanging out on the beach, or even strolling the aisle of a grocery store in a shopping cart.

"Lola is a princess and a ham, to be sure. She loves to travel, go places, and have people tell her she is beautiful," laughed Sandy. "Lola also likes to dress up in all sorts of outfits, but most of all, she loves to eat."

Nothing seems to faze the tiny Lola, who has appeared on television shows, on the cover of magazines, and has even taken part in her own book signing

PHOTO BY Aurora Boyington

◁ Small equines are cute—no butts about it.

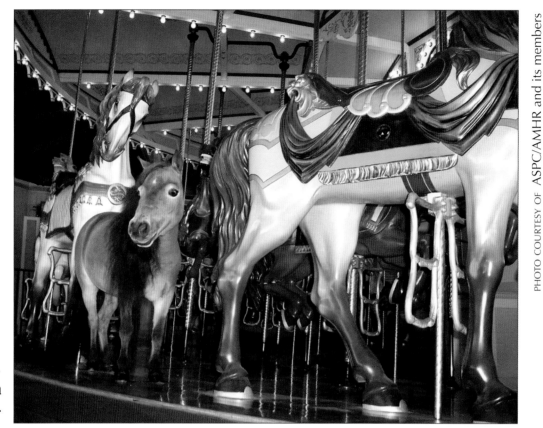

Lola takes a ➤
spin on a
carousel.

at Barnes and Nobles for her book titled *The Wonderful Life of Lola: A Day at the Beach*.

What Lola really excels at, like any good debutante, is having her picture taken. "She has posed for tens of thousands of pictures," Sandy said. "She is so used to posing that if I put her in a situation, she just waits for me to finish taking her picture. In some of her photos, like on the carousel or in the pet store, you will notice she isn't even wearing a halter."

Lola has been the grand prize winner of several photography contests, often beating out hundreds of contestants. "In one of the contests she won a digital camera, which has been put to use capturing her many adventures for all to share," Sandy said.

Thanks to her tiny size and her joy at being the center of attention, Lola has turned into a true ambassador for Miniature Horses. Her many fans have come to love her, and her charisma is truly infectious. "Her size is undeniably unusual and her personality unbeatable," Sandy said.

## Saving a Foal: Savin' A Buck

Sometimes the story of a Miniature Horse comes along that is so heartwarming and adorable that it brings a smile to the faces of all who hear it. Ron and Barbara Johnson of Minnesota have such a story about a tiny Miniature Horse named Bucky that the couple rescued and rehabilitated. And along the way, the special little Miniature captured the heart of Ron, a man who wasn't a big fan of little horses.

Barbara said she was a city girl who always had a passion for horses and always dreamed of owning a Miniature Horse. Her husband Ron, however, grew up on a dairy farm and had little use for horses. "One day while driving on a back road near our home, Ron spotted a Miniature mare and foal. The

⋎ As a foal, Bucky was the same size as the family dog.

PHOTO BY Barbara Johnson

PHOTO BY Barbara Johnson

Sweet little ➢
Bucky gives the
dog a kiss.

foal was unable to stand, and the owner planned to have the colt destroyed," Barbara recalls. "The foal had what appeared to be contracted tendons and had to crawl on his knees to keep up with his mother. Ron asked if he could have the little horse, and the owner agreed. Ron picked him up and carried him from the pasture to the front seat of his pickup truck."

Barbara was thrilled with the idea of having a Miniature Horse of her own but heartbroken at the pathetic condition of the tiny foal. "I really feared getting attached to him, but Ron had a plan. He cut some PVC in half lengthwise and wrapped ace bandages around the foal's fragile legs, stabilizing the legs with PVC and more bandages," Barbara said. "The first time the little horse stood on his braced legs, he gave us the most delightful whinny."

Barbara said Bucky immediately stole Ron's heart, and their bond was undeniable. They named him Savin' A Buck but called him "Bucky" for short. "We worked out an agreement with the previous owner to have Bucky stay with his mother for a few months. We visited him two to three times a day to change his bandages and soak his legs," Barbara said, recalling the bond that grew stronger as the days went by. "When our truck would pull up, Bucky would leave his mother and run as fast as he could to us. He loved Ron, and the feeling was mutual."

Within six weeks Bucky was able to stand without his braces, although his legs were still weak. Ron and Barbara continued their daily visits and watched as Bucky grew stronger and stronger. "Ron and Bucky would race each other in the pasture every evening; it really was a heartwarming sight," Barbara said.

As Bucky grew, Barbara continued to worry about his hooves, so she sent an e-mail out to farriers in Minnesota, complete with photos of Bucky's legs and hooves. "A farrier named Neal Martin from Bemiji, Minnesota, e-mailed back and was such a support to us," Barbara said. "The first time Bucky needed his hooves trimmed, we put him in the back of our pickup with the topper, and I laid in the back with him for the two-hour ride. Neal did his first trim for free and still keeps in touch with us. He is a hero to me."

⋎ Ron Johnson and Bucky share a special father-son moment.

PHOTO BY Barbara Johnson

PHOTO BY Barbara Johnson

⋏ "Hey, Dad, wait up!"

When Bucky was ready to be weaned, Ron and Barbara took him home, where he now lives as a happy two-year-old with several other Miniature Horses that have come to live with Ron and Barbara. "I am so glad that we took a chance on saving Bucky," Barbara said. "And I will always treasure the relationship that Ron and Bucky have developed. It is a beautiful bond."

## Smitten with Small Equines

A great deal of the success and popularity of Shetland Ponies and Miniature Horses in America is due to families who have fallen in love with the small equines and made it their priority to love, raise, show, and promote the breeds. Many families have enjoyed their involvement with Shetland Ponies and Miniature Horses for many generations, with grandparents and parents passing

⋏ A small equine has a hair-raising good time.

on to their children a true love for the remarkable small breeds. It only takes one look at a pint-size pony to melt your heart, and thanks to many families across the country, small-equine lovers everywhere will continue to have those heartwarming moments.

## Roberts Family Ponies

Carolyn and Harold Roberts started their Roberts Family Ponies in South-Central Illinois in the mid 1960s. What started as a desire to own a Shetland Pony for fun has turned into a four-generation pony operation and a love for Shetlands that easily crosses the generation gap. "My family started with pony rides and local parades, then started showing locally," said Amy Roberts Clark, who continues the family Shetland tradition with her own farm called Legacy Shetlands. "Then they started showing nationally and became noted for national champions."

In the early days, the Roberts family had a team of ponies and created a "peddler's wagon" that they drove in local parades and events. Like many people involved with ponies, it wasn't long before they began raising a few ponies under the banner of RFP. "All ponies raised in the Roberts's program still carry the RFP prefix," Amy said. "Today, Roberts Family Ponies are still actively involved with Modern American Shetlands. Moderns are the family's primary interest, although various members of the extended family have been involved with Classic American Shetlands, Foundation Classics, American Show Ponies, and Miniature Horses."

The Roberts Family holds the distinction of being one of the longest-involved families with the American Shetland Pony Club and American Miniature Horse Registry, and for fourteen years Amy has served as

PHOTO BY Jack Schatzberg

Roberts Family ➤ Ponies: Congress and World Grand Champion Modern Mare RFP It's About Time, with Amy Roberts Clark at the whip.

the editor of the registry's magazine, *The Journal*. "My family became involved with the American Shetland Pony Club in 1968, and all four of the Roberts children—who are now adults—have continued their involvement with the ASPC and Modern American Shetlands," Amy said, adding that granddaughter Torrie Roberts shows Moderns, is active in the youth program, and served as ASPC/AMHR Queen in 2002.

While the fourth generation of Modern Shetland enthusiasts is going strong, much of the registry's success is owed to matriarch Carolyn Roberts. Before

PHOTO COURTESY OF THE Roberts Family

◄ Generations of a family: Hannah "Katie" Clark takes part in a leadline class on RFP River of Time, a three-time Congress Grand Champion Modern Mare and Hall of Fame Halter Pony. Katie is being led by Amy Roberts Clark.

See? ➤
Unicorns do exist.

PHOTO BY Bob Langrish

her death, Carolyn served as a national director for the American Shetland Pony Club and helmed the Modern Shetland Committee for several years. Under her leadership, the Modern committee established the Modern Weanling Sweepstakes, a program eventually adapted in some fashion in both the Classic Division and the American Miniature Horse Registry. Carolyn is probably most noted for the complete revamping of the registry's royalty program in the mid 1990s. Today, the ASPC/AMHR still uses the queen, ambassador, and junior royalty program, a program that is instrumental in promoting Shetlands, Miniatures, and the ASPC/AMHR registry.

While the Roberts Family is known for their continued support of the American Shetland Pony Club, they are also known for their champion ponies. Their breeding stock includes Cres-Or-Lar's Prime Time, the sire of multiple World, Congress, Futurity, and All-Star Champion Modern American Shetlands and a Hall of Fame Superior Sire; and Cres-Or-Lar's Lady in Waiting, the dam of multiple World, Congress, Futurity, and All-Star Champion Modern

American Shetlands, and a Hall of Fame Superior Dam. Notable Modern American Shetland Show Champions from the Roberts Family Ponies includes, to name just a few: RFP 6/8 Time, three-time Congress and World Grand Champion, Under Harness; RFP Time For Love, a Multiple World and Congress Grand Champion in both Halter and Roadster and Former Pony of the Year, Double Hall of Fame Halter and Roadster; RFP It's About Time, World and Congress Grand Champion in both Halter and Under Harness, Former Futurity and All-Star Champion, Former Pony of the Year, Hall of Fame Halter;

PHOTO BY Stuart Vesty

◄ A beautiful reflection: Little Kings Buck Echo.

PHOTO BY Washburn Photography

⋀ Pretty as a picture: A Miniature Horse strikes a pose.

RFP River of Time, a three-time Congress Grand Champion Mare, Multiple Congress, World, and All-Star titles; and RFP Time and Temperature, a three-time Congress Grand Champion in Country Pleasure Driving.

"One of the things our family is most proud of are the people we've helped get started with Modern Shetlands," Amy said. "Several folks bought their first pony from us, and some of the noted RFP champions were campaigned by other people. Two of today's up-and-coming young trainers got their start in ponies with RFP stock. With our own fourth generation of Modern Shetland enthusiasts going strong, and with the good friendships of some new farms and young trainers, we hope the RFP presence with American Shetlands—especially Modern—will continue for many, many years."

## Celebrating Little King Farm and Buckeroo

Over thirty years ago, Marianne Eberth of Little King Farm in Indiana bought a Miniature Horse for her children—a decision that changed her life forever. Since then, Marianne has spent three decades raising and showing Miniature Horses and Shetland Ponies and is a leading breeder in the Miniature industry.

"My mom's impact on the Miniature Horse world has been tremendous, as she was one of the first to take the Miniature from an exotic, dwarf-sized toy to what the show horses are today," said Marianne's daughter, Robin. "She purchased the best stallion she could and dedicated her life to him and to producing champions. We now manage approximately four hundred horses during the summer months, and we stand numerous World Grand Champions in halter and driving. We also have about thirty Shetland Ponies, one of which was Congress Pony of the Year, D & S Knight Cap. We

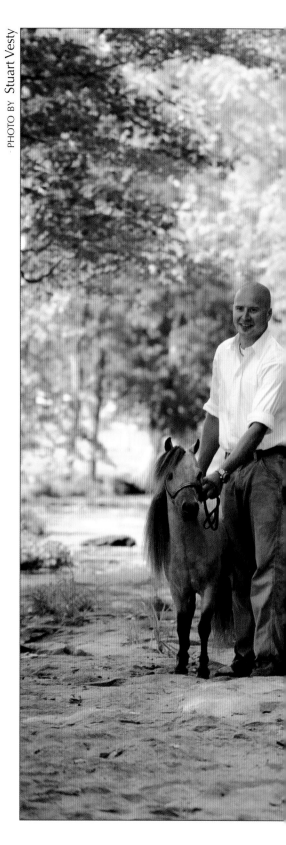

PHOTO BY Stuart Vesty

Miniature Horses are a family tradition at Little King ➤ Farm. Pictured with their World Champion Senior Stallions are (left to right) Brian Eberth with Buck Echo, Heather Eberth Teike with Ima Boones Little Buckeroo Too, Marianne Eberth with Boones Little Buckeroo, Robin Mingione (Eberth) with Little Kings Psyched Up Buck, and John Eberth with Alvadars Double Destiny.

also stand another very famous Shetland stallion on the farm named RFP 6/8 Time, a multiple Congress Champion."

Robin said her mom grew up with Shetland Ponies owned by her grandparents but soon ventured into horses. "They are to blame for her love of horses," Robin said with a laugh, adding that Marianne left big horses behind when she purchased a buckskin Miniature stallion by the name of Buckeroo.

With his stunning looks and unmistakable "look at me" look, Buckeroo has become one of the most well-known Miniature stallions in the world. He has won three National Grand Champion Senior Stallion titles and captured the hearts of Miniature fans everywhere. Buckeroo's long list of champion sons, daughters, grandsons, and granddaughters certainly gives credence to the power of the pedigree. Little King Farm has amazing family photos where

PHOTO BY Stuart Vesty

◄ Ima Boones Little Buckeroo Too shows how handsome he is.

A small equine shows off its beautiful head ➤

each member of the family is holding a look-a-like buckskin, all children or grandchildren of the great Buckeroo.

"Our family is active in the small-equine industry at all levels. We sponsor clinics and seminars and auctions here on the farm for youth, amateurs, and professionals. We still show at the World level every year and participate in the breed any way possible. We help our local clubs as well as the national and international associations," Robin said. "My brothers, sisters, and myself have all served on committees and held offices within the associations. Marianne foals out over a hundred Miniatures each year, and we breed over 150 outside mares each year as well—Shetlands and Miniatures. We have spread the Miniature breed to countries all over the world, including Japan, Australia, New Zealand, South Africa, Mexico, and the majority of Europe."

Marianne has proven to be a dominant force in the Miniature Horse world, and Robin is proud of the legacy her mom has created. "I could write a book just on the horses my mom has produced and their titles. We have consistently won World and National titles each year with our horses or horses we have produced. One of the best testaments to my mom's breeding program is that she has won the Get of Sire award with Boone's Little Buckeroo in 1992, 1993, 1994, and then again in 2007 as Buckeroo. He is the only horse to win three years consecutively only to return over ten years later to win again. My mom has dedicated her life and his life to this breed."

## Emerald Glenn Farm's Pony Passion

Jackie Tyler has fond memories of her first Shetland Pony, a pony that sparked a lifelong passion for Shetlands. "It was around 1959. I was three years old, and the pony came home in the back seat of our station wagon," Jackie recalled. "My great Uncle Henry had to hold him in a gunny sack so he wouldn't soil the car."

Jackie and her husband Mark own Emerald Glenn Farm in Wisconsin, and Jackie believes there is a simple reason why they still have Shetlands today. "They make us smile," she said, adding that she still smiles when she thinks about a Shetland Pony stallion her dad brought home when she was a young girl. "He was a trick pony named Smokey Joe. He'd sit, walk on his hind legs, do everything. He was dead tame. We'd pick every kind of grass, weed, flower, and dandelion and grind them up with chunks of salt block and feed the 'horse stew' to Smokey Joe. Some of the ponies wouldn't eat it, but Smokey Joe would."

Emerald Glenn Farm shows and breeds nationally competitive Shetland Ponies and also promotes the breed on a local level with farm visits, parades, and more. "I got my start in the show pony world from a colorful Irishman named Rollie Flynn. In 1959 my folks bought the first of their Shetlands from Whyte Gates Pony Farm, where Rollie was the trainer. He was the first of many

Here she is: ➢ Trainer Rollie Flynn shows Whyte Gates Miss America as a yearling in 1961. Rollie was the trainer for Whyte Gates Pony Farm, owned by Norman and Clarice McCrea and located in St. Paul, Minnesota, during the pony boom of the 50s and 60s.

important people in my life, and he could do about anything with a pony. Rollie gave me old pony journals, show tack, and lots of insight into conformation, fitting a pony for the show ring, and pony character, something that you don't talk much about today—true pony character. Mrs. Clarice McCrea was the owner of Whyte Gates, and she purchased my first membership to the Shetland Pony Club. I was about eight or nine years old at the time," Jackie said.

Jackie has great memories of ponies from that time period and said that commercial hitches were popular, especially the Bongaard Cheese Company's six-pony hitch that traveled to all the fairs. "Rollie's sons worked their summer jobs on the hitch and traveled all year with it. They even had Dalmatian coach dogs," Jackie recalls. "We were lucky enough to come across the old red Bon-gaard hitch wagon last summer, and it's in our shed today."

After Jackie got married, they didn't have enough money for ponies, and she had to give up her pony dream for a while. "Then in 1996 we bought a farm, and I saw a pony listed in a dairy farm dispersal sale. I called on it and asked about his registration papers. They read them to me, and it was a Warren Hansen pony. I had known Warren from when I was young, so I phoned him and we caught up on old times. And of course I went to the sale and bought the pony. Now we are back full blast in them."

Jackie said she started attending Shetland Congress around the year 2000 and found that certain ponies kept catching her eye. "They were incredible. They were by a pony called Up & Atom and others by a pony called Rock 'E.' I went to work to find out who these ponies were and discovered they were the same strain. Today I refer to them as Rock O's, and they were all offspring of a stallion called Bar G Rock O," Jackie said. "I loved them; they were really a breed of their own. You could pick out one in any herd—they were that distinctive. I focused my attention on acquiring as many of those good ponies as I could afford and wound up owning Atom himself," Jackie said, adding that

PHOTO COURTESY OF Jackie Tyler

◁ Ponies for life: Jackie Tyler of Emerald Glenn Farm began her love for ponies at a very early age. At age ten, Jackie spent a few moments with a filly called Lady and her dog Gelsie.

⚘ Foal nest: Colorful foals at Step-N-Stone Farm enjoy a rest in the hay.

her mentor Linda Seddon of Rhapsody Shetlands has also helped her as she has developed her breeding program. "I think Linda has the best equine eye of anyone I have ever known. She also has the desire to help guide and support a person's dreams."

Thanks to wonderful friends, and a passion for ponies, Jackie is certainly living out her dream—smiling at her ponies all along the way.

## The Colorful Step-N-Stone Farm

In the mid-1990s, Shirlee Busbee was leafing through a copy of *The Encyclopedia of the Horse* when she came across a photo of a jet black American Shetland Pony. Shirlee said it was love at first sight, and she knew she had to have a pony like the one in the picture.

That was the early beginnings of Step-N-Stone Farm, a California farm where Shirlee and her husband Howard breed American Shetland Ponies,

⋏Laurelwood's Katie CHD, owned by Zona Schnieder, with Larry Parnell driving.

predominately pintos. "We started it as a backyard hobby, and now we have a full-blown breeding program that includes ponies that have won championship titles at Shetland Congress," Shirlee said.

"In 1996 we found the pony we were looking for: Sandman Cody's Cinnamon N.T.A. We bought Cinnamon in foal to the Hall of Fame, and now Superior Sire, Scotch Label, with the idea of raising a few registered American Shetland Ponies," Shirlee said. "Before we knew it, we had a filly, Cinnamon's Cayenne Label, winning championships in the show ring and on her way to the Halter Hall of Fame; three brood mares bred back to Scotch Label; and two more Scotch Label foals on the ground."

Step-N-Stone Farm also has a love affair with color, and most of their ponies are double-registered with the American Pinto Association. With all that color it seemed only natural to head to the show ring, and Step-N-Stone started working with Jim Curry of Jim Curry Training Center in Acampo, California. "Under the expert showmanship of Jim, our ponies have been consistent winners in show rings all over the country," Shirlee said.

Shirlee will always be grateful that thanks to a simple photo in a book, the colorful Step-N-Stone was born. "Our ponies are small, but they win big!" Shirlee added.

## Larry Parnell Stables

Larry Parnell, the current president of the American Shetland Pony Club and the American Miniature Horse Registry, started his Larry Parnell Stables in the 1950s, with a focus on training and showing Shetland Ponies. Located in the beautiful foothills of the Ozark Mountains, it seemed like the perfect place to raise ponies.

PHOTO BY Jack Schatzberg

⋏ Larry Parnell drives D&S 21st-Century Thomas at the 2003 AMHR Nationals.

The farm shifted in the 1990s, when Larry and his partner Murl Creel joined forces with the Erwins of NFC Miniature Horse Farm and started showing Miniature Horses. Almost twenty years later, and with more than two hundred National Champions, the Miniature Horse has become a main part of Larry and Murl's lives.

"I've been president of the ASPC/AMHR for almost ten years," Larry said. "I really enjoy seeing and meeting the new people who come into the organization. I like watching them go from having a little horse to having a National Champion."

Larry has between seventy-five and a hundred Shetlands and Miniatures on his farm and said one of his favorite times of the year is foaling season. "I love seeing if what you bred is going to turn out like you expected," he said, adding that every foal is a surprise.

PHOTO COURTESY OF Bellevue Farm Classic Shetlands

◄ A man and his Ponies: Eldon McCall of Bellevue Farm Classic Shetlands enjoys a few minutes with his ponies.

"I got involved with the ponies as a result of my family, and now it's our fiftieth year in business and I still enjoy it. I really like the training end of the horses and ponies. I like taking a green horse and watching it progress," Larry said. "My favorite horse was probably Drummer Boy. I won Nationals with him six times."

## Eldon McCall and Bellevue Farm Classic Shetlands

Eldon McCall grew up with ponies, horses, cows, and an assortment of other animals. "I've always had equines of some sort. My father bought me my first pony when I was two years old," Eldon said. "After I retired from the school system, after thirty-eight years of teaching, my granddaughter asked for a pony. One thing led to another, and here we are today."

When asked how many ponies Eldon has at his Bellevue Farm Classic Shetlands in Iowa, Eldon laughs and speaks like a true horse person. "I don't know. We're foaling now and already have thirteen foals on the ground. When we are done we will have close to thirty foals."

In 1996, Eldon was at a pony sale when he met Vern Benna. The two became friends, and for the Bellevue Farms breeding program, the rest was history. "I really got started in my breeding program when I met Vern. His ponies all carry the VB suffix, and he was the definition of a true pony breeder. He bred many great ponies while using a variety of different stallions."

Eldon also credits John Vriezelaar of Red Rock Pony Farm in Iowa with helping him understand how to have a top-quality breeding program. "I've had a lot of Red Rock ponies, and that's what we breed today," he said.

Although Eldon is seventy-five years old, he is savvy in the horse world and said the Internet has really changed the way he sells ponies. "All we do is breed and sell ponies, and as soon as we list the sale ponies on the Internet, the phone starts ringing, because our goal is to breed really good ponies," he said. "We sell our ponies to people all across the country."

Thanks to his granddaughter wanting a pony, the McCall family has found a lifelong passion in ponies. "We really enjoy the breeding part. Both of my sons work with me. It's a family affair, and it's all fun."

## Taylor Pony Farm: Raising Ponies and Families

The Taylor Pony Farm, located in Ohio, has been raising American Shetland Ponies for over sixty years. While they started by showing grade ponies at county fairs in the 1940s, their main joy surrounding the ponies was that it was a great way for the family to enjoy life together.

Over the years the Taylor Pony Farm has successfully shown in Modern, Classic, and Miniatures, while also enjoying a prosperous breeding program. For over forty years they have also hosted an annual production sale. "We have always tried to raise kids' ponies with good conformation, with the hope of making kids happy and keeping families together, with each other and

⅄ Cute kids: Abbie and Samuel E. Taylor competing.

All grown up: ➤
Abbie Taylor, of
Taylor Pony Farm, has
shown since she was
a little girl.

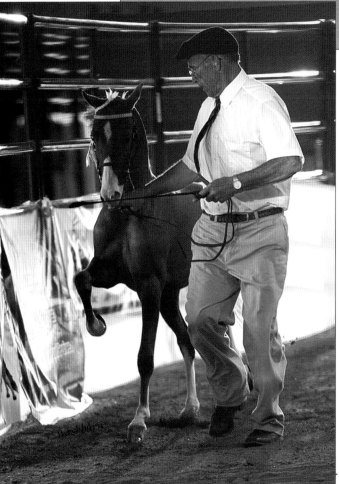

the ponies," the Taylor family said.

Dr. Thomas J. Taylor is a veterinarian and currently runs the Taylor Pony Farm operation. His father started the farm in 1945 when he moved his wife and three children—one of them young Tom—to the country. He bought

◄ Taylor Pony Farm: Dr. Thomas Taylor has spread his love of ponies to his children.

Tom and his brother and sister a Shetland Pony, and the Taylor Pony Farm was born.

Tom's father enjoyed driving teams and drove for over thirty-seven years. Tom's mother, Mary, was the one who decided that the Taylor Pony Farm should add a prefix to their ponies' names—something that would distinguish their ponies from others. While Tom's dad thought that "Wolverines" was a good name because he had graduated from the University of Michigan, Mary thought it sounded odd—plus she had gone to Michigan State. Soon the prefix "Michigan" was added to the ponies' names, and it continues today—even though the farm has moved to Ohio.

## They Started Small

### International Dressage Competitor George Williams

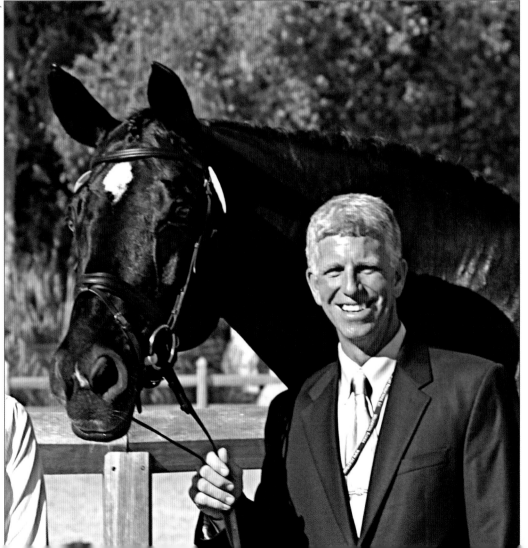

PHOTO COURTESY OF THE Williams Family

◁ International dressage rider George Williams and his partner Rocher.

PHOTO COURTESY OF THE Williams Family

George William's ➤ dreams to represent the United States began on the back of his Shetland Pony Goldie.

George Williams has ridden at the top of the competitive dressage world for many years and has represented the United States in the World Cup in Sweden and in Germany. In addition, George gives back to the horse community by serving on several committees for the United States Dressage Federation, including serving as vice president for many years. While George may be best known for his winning partnership with the black Westfalen mare Rocher, George started out on a much smaller mount.

George laughs when he remembers his first pony, a Shetland named Mitzi. "I would use a ladder to climb up her rump and get on her," George said. "My family purchased her when my oldest sister, who was sixteen years older than me, was only five. There were nine children in my family, and Mitzi was my sister's first pony and my first pony and the first pony of each of the seven kids in between."

◄ A young George Williams takes it upon himself to find inventive ways to mount his Shetland Pony Mitzi.

Mitzi died when George was only five years old, but he said he still has great riding memories of the little Shetland. "We were never certain of her age, but she was probably around thirty when she died," he said.

One of George's most vivid memories of Mitzi was her ability to unseat her rider in the woods. "We lived in New Hampshire, far from town, on a farm that was mostly woods and rocks and boulders. We did a lot of trail riding, and we had a favorite trail in the woods that was up a hill between my parents' place and my grandparents' place. It was a trail that Mitzi knew well. There was a point on the trail where she had her own 'special' path that she liked to take which had an especially low branch on it. She could easily fit under the branch, but it left no room for the rider," George recalls. "No matter how determined you were, you could not dissuade her from taking this path. Mitzi always waited on the other side of the branch for the rider to catch her and get back on. Despite this routine, I remember spending many enjoyable hours riding Mitzi."

After Mitzi passed away, the Williams family bought a registered Shetland Pony named Sky Farm's Golden Carla. "We called her 'Goldie Who Sat in a Bucket of White Paint' because she had a white rump," George said.

Riding Goldie was a turning point in the young rider's life, and George vividly remembers the day that—thanks to Goldie—he began to dream about representing the United States as a dressage rider. "I was in Pony Club in 1964, and the district commissioner of our Pony Club held a mock Olympics in the spirit of the Mexico City Olympics. I chose to represent Mexico, and I proudly rode down the center line for my entrance. I halted at X, saluted, and Goldie seized that moment to put her head down and eat grass. I was unsuccessful in bringing her head up and unceremoniously burst into tears," George said. "I was excused, and to this day I still have no memory of how I eventually left the arena. Needless to say, Mexico did not do well in those Olympics. But that experience with Goldie was the start of my dream to compete internationally for the United States. Part of my dream was realized nearly forty years later when I first represented the United States in the 2003 World Cup in Gothenburg, Sweden, on the wonderful mare Rocher."

## Best-selling Mystery Writer Tami Hoag

George Williams isn't the only well-known dressage rider that began his career on the back of an adorable Shetland Pony. *New York Times* best-selling mystery writer Tami Hoag is also a successful Grand Prix rider. Tami, who has thrilled countless fans with her fourteen best-selling suspenseful mysteries, was thrilled with ponies from

PHOTO COURTESY OF Tami Hoag

Tami Hoag and her Shetland Pony Dan ➤ were an inseparable team.

the beginning. "I asked my parents for a pony every chance I got," Tami remembers.

Tami started her riding life on a pony named Smoky, but it was a Shetland Pony named Dan that won her heart

and made her a lifelong horse lover. "I loved Dan the Pony," Tami recalls fondly, adding that the small pinto Shetland taught her joy and confidence.

That confidence has come in handy. Tami is now an amateur Grand Prix dressage rider, riding at the top of the sport. The elegant horses Tami rides and competes today may be a far cry from little Dan, but that doesn't keep Tami from remembering Dan as her best friend and inseparable buddy.

"Dan was a wise old soul and would never do anything he believed was beyond my capability as a rider," Tami said. "For the first year I had him, he would *not* canter. No matter how I tried to coax him, irritate him, beg him, bribe him, he absolutely would not canter—until I became a better rider with better balance and was in no danger of just falling off."

Tami believes it was her constant companion Dan the Pony that shaped her into the rider—and also the writer—she is today. Two of Tami's bestselling novels, *Dark Horse* and *Alibi Man*, are based in the horse world, a world

PHOTO COURTESY OF Tami Hoag

that began with an ice cream–eating, hat-wearing, cart-pulling pony named Dan. "He was the perfect pony with a heart of gold," Tami said. "I was lucky to have the pony that every child dreams about and hopes to own."

Tami said part of owning her dream pony including riding him all over town bareback, while dreaming of owning a

◁ Dan and Tami Hoag earned money to buy Dan a saddle by selling advertising on the side of Dan's pony cart.

*New York Times* bestselling mystery writer Tami Hoag began her riding career on a pony but has since moved on to larger mounts.

PHOTO COURTESY OF Tami Hoag

saddle. "I learned to hitch Dan up myself and drove him all over town. I drove him in parades and hung advertising for local businesses on my cart, which earned me money to save up for a new saddle," Tami said, laughing as she remembered her goal of buying a saddle. "When I had saved up almost a hundred dollars—a fortune to a nine-year-old—I became obsessed with the idea of the new saddle. My oldest brother was getting married around that time, and one weekend my mother was going to go shopping with his fiancée to look for a dress. When I overheard them planning to go to a bridal shop, I got all excited and asked, 'Do you think they might have saddles, too?' Typical horse-crazy little girl, that was all I could think about."

## World and National Reining Champions Jon and Seth Ingram

Jon and Seth Ingram are a father-and-son duo that hold World and National Reining Championship titles and have dedicated their lives to training and showing horses. While today they focus on reining horses at their Ingram

PHOTO COURTESY OF Ingram Training Stable

◄ Jon Ingram started on a Shetland Pony before becoming a National Reining Champion.

Training Stables in Loxahatchee, Florida, both learned to ride on Shetland Pony crosses.

Jon grew up in Southern California, where his childhood included riding his Shetland-Mustang cross named Smoky everywhere, including the mountains. "I had so much fun riding him in the mountains and in gymkhanas, and I even rode Smoky to school," Jon recalls, adding that he spent his summers at his uncle's farm and broke his first horse when he was only ten.

Smoky was the perfect pony for a little cowboy, and Jon still smiles when he thinks about the tricks he taught Smoky. "I taught him to rear just like Trigger," he said. "I also taught him to kick out at aggressive dogs. All I had to do was slap him on the rump."

Jon's entire life has been devoted to horses, so it was only

PHOTO COURTESY OF Ingram Training Stable

◄ Seth Ingram shows off his roping style on his pony Sugar Bear.

Lucas (left) and Seth ➤
Ingram stand in the shadow of
the world's largest steer.

PHOTO COURTESY OF Ingram Training Stable

natural that his son Seth would follow in his father's footsteps. By the time he was four years old, Jon was riding two Shetland crosses—Snappy Tom and Sugar Bear. "Snappy Tom was a great reining pony. He had been the Nevada State Reining Champion pony, and he wore a little silver bit that was made especially for him," Jon said.

Sugar Bear was also a great pony and allowed Jon the opportunity to rope with the adults. "I have reached the Top Ten in the National Reining Horse Association and have traveled a lot and met great people," Jon said. "But I will always look back fondly on riding those ponies.

## Television Star Carson Kressley

Television star and style guru Carson Kressley is a fashion and design expert, a fact television viewers embraced on Carson's shows *Queer Eye for the Straight Guy* and *How to Look Good Naked*. With his great sense of humor and unde-niable sense of style, Carson is a fashion force, starring in movies, designing his own clothing line, and writing the fashion books *Queer Eye for the Straight*

◄ Television star Carson Kressley takes a ride on one of his grandparents' many ponies at Kressley's Pony Farm.

*Guy* and *Off the Cuff*, as well as the cartoon-inspired book *You're Different and That's Super*.

While fashion is his passion, Carson is a dedicated equestrian who began his career on a Shetland Pony—or actually on hundreds of them. Carson grew up next door to his grandparents and their Kressley's Pony Farm in rural Pennsylvania and said he has great memories of growing up with Shetland Ponies, Hackneys, and Miniature Horses, who were definitely his best friends.

"There were always a multitude of ponies and Minis to ride and drive—how lucky was I?! I just had to walk out the door and jump on, which I did often, and not always with the best results," Carson said with a laugh. "Both my grandparents are no longer with us, but they gave me the most precious gift I could ever ask for, a pony—or the choice of a hundred when I was a child—and a lifelong love of horses. In fact, when people visit my home today, an apartment on Park Avenue in New York City, about a hundred miles away from Kressley's Pony Farm in rural Pennsylvania, they are greeted by a nearly life-sized painting of a palomino Shetland Pony, with a plaque that bears the name KRESSLEY'S PERFECTION. It is my most prized possession."

Carson's grandparents, the late Ralph and Pauline Kressley, started breeding ponies in the 1940s. "It was the classic story," Carson said. "My grandmother bought a pony for my dad when he was a little boy, and he took little or no interest. But she absolutely loved them. My grandparents became one of the largest breeders in the country of Shetlands and Hackneys."

Carson said he fondly remembers his early years, flying to Georgia or driving to Ohio to attend the sales with his grandparents. When his grandparents started to focus on Miniature Horses, they bought a golden palomino named Kressley's Little Rascal as the herd sire for their operation.

"We lived out in the country, and my siblings were much older than me, so there were not a lot of other kids to play with," Carson said. "So I just hung out at the barn or in the pastures or sat in the well-worn feed troughs listening to the contented munching of a herd of ponies eating their dinner. I don't think there's a more peaceful sound in the world."

Throughout the years, Carson has continued to show a commitment to the small equine breeds he loved so

Carson Kressley filming a video segment ➤ for the ASPC/AMHR called "Today's Shetland Pony" and "Think Big . . . Go Small."

PHOTO COURTESY OF ASPC/AMHR and its members

dearly as a child, hosting two shows for the American Shetland Pony Club and American Miniature Horse Registry: "Today's Shetland Pony" and "Think Big . . . Go Small with American Miniature Horses."

While Carson stays busy in the celebrity and fashion worlds, he hasn't left his love for equines behind. When he was in his teens, his grandmother bought him a Saddlebred, and Carson has been devoted to the breed ever since. "We show on the same circuit as the Hackneys, and when I see them I am always nostalgic about my family's heritage in the pony business," Carson said. "We have owned several top road ponies but mostly still own and show Saddlebreds. In 2008 I reached the highlight of my career when I was Reserve World Champion in the Amateur Fine Harness Division at the World Championship Horse Show in Louisville, Kentucky. Now my eleven-year-old niece is riding ponies and showing Saddlebreds too. And it all started with a Shetland Pony!"

PHOTO COURTESY OF Janet Lewis

◄ Pen Lewis was the final Lewis child to show on Aloysius, the perfect family show pony.

Trip cuts a dashing ➢
figure on Aloysius.

## An Entire Family Learns to Ride on Aloysius, the Perfect Family and Show Pony

Sometimes a very special pony comes along that has a lasting impact on a whole family, and an American Shetland Pony named Woodcock Aloysius, standing at only 10 hands, was such a pony. Owned by Janet and Jonathan Lewis, a New Hampshire family with eight children, Aloysius taught all eight Lewis children to ride and spent over twenty years showing with the Lewis children. Along the way, the little pony earned a staggering 750 trophies, countless ribbons, and enough silver for a queen—not to mention lots of fans and an enormous following in the press.

To say that Aloysius was a legend in the horse show world would be an understatement. From local shows to the prestigious National Horse Show,

Aloysius won it all, taking his pint-size riders along for the ride of a lifetime. While the small, dappled gray Shetland was a legend in the show ring, he was also a beloved member of the Lewis family for thirty years—a bond that began on Christmas morning in 1955 when neighbors showed up at the Lewis family home with Aloysius, a Shetland weanling, in their arms and gave him to the Lewis family.

Janet had always wanted a pony and was pleased when they were given Aloysius, knowing her children would grow up with a pony. No one could have imagined, however, that Aloysius would turn out to be a pony that could safely cart a four-year-old rider around the ring at a show, drive a cart in a parade, and then turn around and head to Madison Square Garden to the equitation finals or on to win the title of Best Pleasure Pony at the Royal Horse Show in Toronto, Canada.

Throughout Aloysius's career, he competed in the Pet Pony division, as well as in the Pet Pony under Harness, Trail Pony, and Model Pet Pony divisions. "Sometimes we would put Aloysius in a pleasure class that included

PHOTO BY Washburn Photography

◁ Janet Lewis is back in the show ring today with her Modern Shetland Pony Cappuccino.

A tiny rider, ➢
Sam Lewis, shows
Aloysius with confidence.

PHOTO COURTESY OF THE Lewis Family

both horses and ponies. Often there would be as many as twenty exhibitors. Aloysius and his rider were perfection and very hard to beat," Janet recalled. "Week after week, year after year, Aloysius continued to make headlines. Horse shows have many classes, and each class had a winner, but the one the reporters and photographers always chose to highlight in the newspapers was Aloysius, an endearing pony, and his young riders."

Janet saved the newspaper clippings, including Aloysius's retirement ceremony at the New Hampshire Deerfield Fair in 1977, and compiled them into a two-hundred-page book for her children and grandchildren. "It is rare that an entire family—as well as many others—have their lives touched so profoundly by one individual, especially when that individual comes in the form of one very special little Shetland Pony," Janet said. "Aloysius was a little pony with a giant heart and an enormous amount of magic."

PHOTO COURTESY OF THE Lewis Family

⋏ Sam Lewis keeps up the family tradition by winning more blue ribbons with Aloysius.

Janet fondly recalls the magical moment in 1968 when they took Aloysius to the largest horse show in North America, the Royal Horse Show in Canada. Aloysius and Janet's daughter, Nifty, were competing, and when they got to the side of the ring they had quite a shock. The other twenty-three ponies in the class were beautiful, large, hunter-type ponies. "We looked as though we didn't belong because Aloysius was a 10-hand Shetland Pony," Janet said, remembering how Aloysius looked so tiny in the big ring, while the other ponies passed by him quickly. "When they lined up I thought Aloysius looked cute, but I still thought he might be in the wrong class!"

While the ponies and riders waited for the results, a brass band played and a thirty-foot red carpet was rolled out. The show dignitaries walked the carpet and stood waiting for the results. Finally the announcer said, "The first place ribbon and trophy in this class of fine ponies goes to Aloysius, ridden by Nifty Lewis from Bedford, New Hampshire."

Janet said she can still remember her heart leaping in her chest at the sound of his name over the loudspeaker, and the response from the crowd was tremendous. "All of the ponies left the arena except Aloysius, and he made the best victory pass ever. He loved the loud, jazzy band that was keeping time with his animated trot, and the cheering and applause was deafening," Janet said. "Once again he had won the heart of a new judge and of every person in that packed coliseum."

While Janet has had plenty of children and grandchildren to keep her busy over the last twenty-five years, she continued to long for another pony. A few years ago she called the American Shetland Pony Club to inquire about finding another Shetland, and that was when she discovered the Modern Shetland breed. Soon a Modern Shetland named Cappuccino came to live with her. At seventy-four years of age, Janet is back in the ring—this time she is showing Cappuccino in the driving divisions and having the time of her life.

"Ponies leave hoof prints on your heart," Janet says with fondness, thinking of the Shetland breed that has been a part of her life for so long and, thanks to her new pony Cappuccino, will continue to do so for years to come.

Robin Moore and her best friend Chub. ➤

PHOTO COURTESY OF Robin Moore

A young ➤
Robin Moore takes a
break to read a book
on her boy-hating
pony Chub.

## World Equestrian Brand's Robin Moore and Her Boy-Hating Shetland Pony

Robin Moore has fond memories of growing up with her Shetland Pony named Chub, but her most vivid recollection is that Chub was a boy hater. "Chub was not a big fan of boys. He would let all the girls ride him, but as soon as a boy got on he would buck him right

Robin Moore, brand manager for World Equestrian ➤
Brands, poses with the Trakehner stallion Halbgott,
owned by dressage rider Marco Bernal.

HALBGOTT
APPROVED STALLION

off," Robin said. "He was my secret weapon if a boy thought he was great—I would just let him ride Chub."

Robin, a brand manager for World Equestrian Brands, started her equestrian life at the age of four, and horses continue to be an integral part of her life. "My dad died when I was only a year old, and when I was four I can remember a good friend of my dad's coming up the street with this pony," Robin said. "He stopped in front of me and said, 'Here's your pony.' That's how I got Chub, who was in his twenties at the time and lived until his forties."

Growing up in Connecticut, Robin lived in a fairytale pony world where Chub was her best friend and confidant. "Thanks to Chub, I had no fear," Robin said. "Luckily for me, Chub was also my mode of transportation. He was just like a bicycle; I rode him everywhere from the time I was very small."

Riding him everywhere included trips to cut down Christmas trees in the winter or to a friend's house for the afternoon, memories that now make Robin smile. "Having a pony from such a young age sealed the deal on my love of horses for my entire life," Robin said. "I would spend hours and hours with Chub; he was a great companion. Plus, when I was with Chub I felt like I was on a big fancy horse, which makes me laugh now that I look back on it—but when you are a kid the world has a different perspective."

Lots of horses came and went in Robin's life after she outgrew Chub, but none were ever as magical as her Shetland Pony. "Chub occupied all of my time. He was an amazing pony—it didn't get any better than him," Robin said.

# The American Shetland Pony Club and the American Miniature Horse Registry: Big Support for Small Equines

The American Shetland Pony Club is often referred to as one of the oldest and the boldest equine registries in the United States. The registry's ability to improve and expand the breed, combined with the enduring qualities of the small equines themselves, are factors that contribute to the breed's longevity. For these reasons the American Shetland Pony Club and the American Miniature Horse Registry have withstood the test of time. Started in 1888, the American Shetland Pony Club is one of the oldest equine registries in the United States. Incorporated in 1972, the American Miniature Horse Registry was the first registry for Miniature Horses in the United States and continues to be one of the foremost organizations committed to the

◄ Becky McKeith driving T.A.M's As Good As It Gets, the 2008 National Grand Champion Modern Shetland Fine Harness.

preservation and promotion of these small equines. Since its inception in the late 1800s, the American Shetland Pony Club has been committed to preserving the lineage and promoting the advancement of these small equines.

Shetland Pony shows, sales, and exhibitions have been popular attractions in the United States for well over a hundred years. In the last decade, the Club and its members have taken a proactive role in keeping their small equines in the public eye.

The American Shetland Pony Club and the American Miniature Horse Registry host annual awards programs to reward top Shetland Ponies and Miniature Horses who compete in sanctioned shows. The club recognizes top breeders, competitors, and national All-Star and Hall of Fame winners at their annual convention.

PHOTO BY Washburn Photography

Tiny Tymes For ➤ Sure Man at the AMHR Miniature Nationals driven by Becky McKeith.

PHOTO BY Liz McMillan

A small equine shows off his ➤ amazing color.

ᐱ Gary Brumm wins the futurity.

In addition, the American Shetland Pony Club also sponsors programs to reward outstanding small equines that excel in events open to all breeds. One example of this is the $10,000 scholarship offered annually to any registered American Shetland Pony who earns the title of Champion Small Pony Hunter at the USEF National Pony Finals.

The USEF National Pony Finals Championships have become the most esteemed competition of their kind in the United States. The Small Hunter Pony is a three-phase competition judging the pony's conformation, way of moving under saddle, and jumping ability. This competition tests many young riders' abilities to compete their ponies over a technical and demanding jump course. To be eligible for the $10,000 scholarship prize, the Champion Small Pony Hunter must be registered with the American Shetland Pony Club (ASPC), and the owner and rider must be current members of the ASPC at the time of the win. In addition, the winning pony must measure within the ASPC height limit of forty-six inches at the withers.

While the club sponsors programs to promote small equines on a national level, individual owners actively promote at the grassroots level. Shetland

⅄ The freedom and beauty of the Liberty class.

PHOTO BY Washburn Photography

⌃ Showing Shetland Ponies is a family affair.

Ponies and Miniature Horses draw crowds at horse expos, state fairs, and parades. Miniature Horse driving drill teams at the Rose Bowl Parade in California and Shetland and Miniatures troops in the Chicago Thanksgiving Day Parade are always crowd pleasers. Owners of small equines throughout North America participate in a number of local parades and expositions to help spread the word about these magnificent animals.

Who says ponies can't fly? ➤

## Miniature Horses Parade through Downtown Chicago

Lennie Bertrand's Miniature Horses know how to wow a crowd, and that is exactly what they do when they march in the annual Thanksgiving Day Parade in downtown Chicago. Lennie, owner of Bertrand's Miniature Horse Ranch in Illinois, and over twenty of his Miniature Horses march in the parade each year, much to the delight of the 400,000-plus spectators who enjoy Chicago's favorite tradition.

PHOTO BY Washburn Photography

◄ The beauty of showing a small equine.

PHOTO BY Washburn Photography

↗ You're never too young to show a Shetland.

◄ Children of all ages can take part in driving, a big benefit of a small equine.

◄ Trainer Belinda Bagby at the head of the class.

Lennie's Minis have participated in the Chicago Thanksgiving parade for eleven years. Lennie said friends from as far away as California, Georgia, and Ohio call and tell him they saw his small equines marching down Chicago's State Street. The parade, which is televised in over seventy-five million homes, gives viewers all across the country the chance to enjoy the Miniature Horses. "The parade organizers hold an informal poll at the end of the parade in which they ask the fans which parade group they like the best, and last year our Miniature Horses came in second," Lennie said. "We were the second favorite behind the Budweiser Clydesdales, but it's tough to beat the Clydesdales."

Lennie believes in reaching out to the community, which is why his family has made it a tradition to invite city children to help lead the Miniature Horses along the parade route. "It's also fun and interesting for the fans because we let them reach out and pet the Minis," Lennie said. "A lot of people have never had the opportunity to touch a horse, especially ones so little."

Strutting their stuff in the Chicago parade is a great way for Miniature Horses to show their versatility and act as ambassadors for the breed. "We have to get up at 2:30 in the morning to take part in the parade, but it's worth it to see how excited the kids get. The Miniatures are so little, and the kids along the parade route aren't scared of them," Lennie said.

The Thanksgiving Day Parade showcases a variety of equestrian breeds and groups, and while the big Clydesdales may impress the parade-goers, it is the small equines that win the hearts of the spectators. "We are one of the few horse groups that are asked back every year," Lennie said.

PHOTO BY Cathy Franks

⋏ Michigan's Nallah, a Modern Shetland Pony owned by Robert and Cathy Franks, shows off her frosted muzzle.

PHOTO BY Cathy Franks

For three consecutive years, Shetland Ponies and Miniature Horses performed exhibitions and transported dignitaries into the arena for the National Horse Show. Mayors, show chairpersons, and even Santa Claus have made their grand appearance driven by teams of Shetlands and Miniatures. When the National Horse Show moved from Madison Square Garden in New York City to Wellington, Florida, twenty-nine Shetland Ponies and Miniature Horses opened the National Horse Show, each carrying a letter on their sides to read W-E-L-C-O-M-E T-O T-H-E N-A-T-I-O-N-A-L H-O-R-S-E S-H-O-W. The crowds cheered as the tiny greeters strutted their stuff.

◄ Michigan's Fox Fire enjoys a romp in the snow.

# A CHAMPION AMONG SMALL EQUINES: MARVIN MCCABE

For over a decade, Ohio-based pony breeder and trainer Marvin McCabe and his family have served as ambassadors to the breed. In an official capacity, Marvin has served several terms on the ASPC/AMHR board and chaired several committees over the years. He was president of the ASPC/AMHR for several years, and he is currently the chairman of the United States Equestrian Federation's Shetland Committee. He actively promotes both Shetlands and Miniature Horses within the USEF. Marvin also single-handedly promotes the World Show held in conjunction with the Ohio State Fair. From signage to flags, to youth prizes and pizza parties, to hosting breakfasts and dinners for competitors, Marvin goes all out to draw attention to small equines at the World Show.

⋎ Marvin McCabe is a driving force in the Shetland Pony and Miniature Horse world.

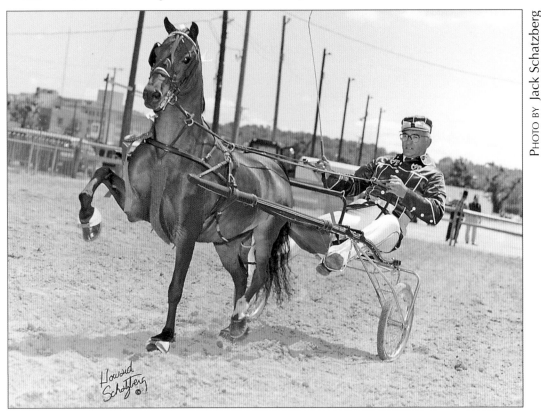

PHOTO BY Jack Schatzberg

Photo by Cathy Franks

⋏ Michigan's Nallah plays in the snow.

"We invite competitors from all the breeds at the show to dine with us at the World Show," explains McCabe. "They get to meet people from the breed and share horse stories. And it isn't long before they are spilling out to barns to see our Shetlands and Miniatures." Marvin's efforts have lead to converts from other breeds purchasing their first small equines at, or shortly after, the show.

While the World Show is certainly one of Marvin's pet projects, his participation in the Shetland Review at the Kentucky Horse Park has consistently produced a showstopper. For more than ten years, Marvin has served as the Shetland and Miniature consultant to the Kentucky Horse Park, and each year he has provided small equines for the annual Parade of Breeds finale, "The Shetland Review." "We started out bringing mares with foals, then added riding and driving ponies, and eventually a Miniature Horse hitch," said Marvin. "At the end we go to the rail and answer questions from the spectators. Many visitors from foreign countries have never seen American Shetland Ponies, and they have lots of questions." In recent years Marvin's "Modern Shetland Review" has included Modern Shetlands in hand as well as driving in pleasure roadster and harness pony equipment. "When you explain what the different types are, it gets people really interested in attending one of our shows." No doubt Marvin suggests they visit his baby, the World Show in Ohio!

## Growing Popularity

From 2005 to 2007, the ASPC and AMHR produced and aired four one-hour television shows and also created a series of television commercials to spread the word about small equines. Even more important, Miniature Horses and Shetland Ponies began showing up in numerous television and print advertising campaigns. Financial institutions, fashion designers, air conditioning companies, beverage companies, communication companies, and others have discovered that small equines can attract big attention to their products. But using endearing small equines to promote sales is certainly not a new idea. In the 1950s and 60s, several Shetland Pony hitches toured the country, attracting attention. Probably the most famous was the Curtiss Candy Company's six-pony hitch out of Gary, Illinois. With five Shetland Pony hitches traveling the United States and one kept at their home base for promotions, it is hard to determine who did the most for whom. While the Shetland Pony hitches drew

The Classic Shetland Pony Graham's Supreme King, owned by  ➤
Tom Graham, bids farewell to the camera.

a lot of attention to the Curtiss Candy Company, the candy company also did a great deal to promote the Shetland Pony's popularity.

The association has also been helpful in supplying footage and photos for a number of television shows and books being produced around the world. There is little doubt that the American Shetland Ponies and Miniature Horses have garnered a great deal of interest around the globe.

In addition, Miniature Horses and Shetland Ponies have also been active helpers in fundraising. These small equines are just the right size to join the on-air crews for telethons to raise money for everything from public television to the Humane Society. Small equines tug at viewers' heartstrings and get them to "pony up" for a number of good causes.

## Oh Mercy, A Mini in the Elevator

Miniature Horses have proven they are wonderful pets, but one particular black pinto, A-division-registered American Miniature mare named Haligonian Mercy Bo Cool—known as Mercy to her family and friends—goes far beyond pet status. Mercy is a television star, has been featured in several books and has been inducted into the American Miniature Horse Registry Hall of Fame for Halter Obstacle, Hunters, and Jumpers.

While she has attained a level of celebrity, Mercy's most amazing attribute is her work as a therapy horse. Mercy is certified as a Delta Society Pet Partner therapy horse and went through her testing with a canine tester who was thrilled and awed at the small equine. "Before she began her test as a therapy pet, I was told that, just like dogs that make a mess, she would be automatically excused if she made a mess," said Mercy's owner Denise Pullis of New York. "Mercy was so wonderful that by the end of the testing, the handler asked if Mercy was available during the day to visit the kids she worked with, along with her therapy dog."

Haligonian Mercy Bo Cool, known as Mercy to her family and friends, ➤ is a therapy horse and a celebrity.

PHOTO BY Cathy Franks

⚔ Graham's Supreme King, a Classic Shetland Pony, shows off his wild side with his wild mane.

Mercy and Denise have spent the past fourteen years volunteering Mercy's services to nursing homes, civic events, parades, fundraisers, and events that help kids with cancer. "The nursing home staff often does a double take when they see a horse in the elevator going to a different floor," Denise said. "Residents ask to have Mercy visit them at their bedsides, kids with cancer run up and hug her around her neck, and people who see her always smile."

Three of Mercy's five foals have followed in their mother's footsteps and become service Minis: Two are permanent residents at different preschools in Massachusetts, and one is in the city of Rochester. "In our early years together, I didn't own a horse trailer, but Mercy, at thirty-three-and-a-half inches tall, was perfectly comfortable jumping into the prepared area of our Jeep Cherokee and traveling by car to events. Her foals often traveled with her this way as well," Denise said. "While this is not a way I advocate shipping horses for

PHOTO BY Darcia Korvarik

⋀ Shetlands and Miniatures may be small, but there is still lots to love.

safety reasons, with careful training it did work very well for Mercy, thanks to her unbelievably willing nature."

Mercy's celebrity status has extended to television appearances, including appearing on a telethon for the Humane Society at Lollypop Farm in Fairport, New York. "The goal was to raise $194,000 that night, and they raised $205,000, surpassing their goal," Denise said. "We charged $1 for a Mercy 'kiss' and not only were children coming up for a kiss, but the reporters from the television station were asking for one as well. Mercy made four television appearances that night, and people told me, 'We saw the little horse on TV and came right down to see her.'"

Mercy also appeared as a Celebrity Horse at the 2006 Equine Affaire in Massachusetts, where she was in stellar company with the equine movie stars from *Seabiscuit* and *Lord of the Rings*. Mercy fascinated audiences with her tricks. She is trained to retrieve items on command, answer yes and no to questions, shake hands, give kisses, and bow. Despite being the smallest horse on Celebrity Row, there was no doubt that her presence was larger than life.

The bond between Denise and Mercy is heartwarming, and Denise is quick to call Mercy an equine prodigy. "I had owned 'big' horses prior to being married and having children, but when I was trying to save for a house, boarding a big horse was not part of the equation. I was introduced to Miniature Horses and just had to have one."

## Andrew and Zig-Zag Fight for a Cure

Arizona Miniature Horse owner Andrew Jentlie grew up riding and showing Minis, including his favorite Mini, Zig-Zag. Active members of the America Miniature Horse Registry, Andrew and his family participated in local parades, community events, and Mini Horse shows and also took their Minis to elementary schools, pediatric dentists, and to visit seniors.

Andrew Jentlie shares a kiss with his favorite Miniature Horse Zig-Zag.

At age nine, however, Andrew's life changed forever when he was diagnosed with Type 1 diabetes. "The weekend Andrew was diagnosed, we also had a mare deliver our first Miniature baby," recalls Andrew's mom, Denice Jentlie. "We decided the moment the foal was born that our small Mini farm would be named Mini Distractions, and we would become more involved with using our Minis to bring smiles to a larger number of people and to help find a cure for diabetes."

It took Andrew a while to adjust to his life with diabetes, but through it all he had Zig-Zag to rely on for comfort and friendship. With the help of his friends, family, and Miniature Horses, Andrew began raising money to help find a cure for diabetes.

When Andrew learned about a charity ball and auction to benefit the Juvenile Diabetes Research Foundation in Phoenix, he made the difficult decision to auction Zig-Zag off to raise money for diabetes. Andrew and his family took Zig-Zag to the black tie affair that was attended by almost nine hundred people, and two families pooled their resources to purchase Zig-Zag for a winning bid of $6,000. Andrew was ecstatic about the amount of money raised by

Zig-Zag, but even more ecstatic by the condition the winning families insisted upon—Zig-Zag would stay with Andrew.

When a thrilled Andrew heard the announcement, he turned to his mother and said, "We're stuck together like glue forever."

The news about Andrew and Zig-Zag made the headlines, and Denice said the emotional experience had a wonderful upside. "The charity ball raised $2.1 million," she said, adding that the benefit would long be remembered for Andrew and his best friend—Zig-Zag the Miniature Horse.

# AN INTERNATIONAL GOODWILL GESTURE

In 2008, the American Shetland Pony Club went global with an international goodwill gesture: presenting the Hong Kong Equestrian Federation with a gift of two American Shetland Ponies to salute their efforts in hosting the Equestrian Olympics.

When reading about the mammoth efforts that the Hong Kong Equestrian Federation put forth to build an Olympic equestrian venue in Hong Kong,

寺蘭小馬
Shetland Ponies

⋏ The American Shetland Pony Club donated two American Shetland Ponies, PC Karmel Kid and FMF Imagination, to the Hong Kong Equestrian Federation.

PHOTO BY Johnny Robb

the ASPC marketing director also read that there were only a few ponies in Hong Kong, imported by the local riding schools, to be used as school ponies. The idea to donate two American Shetland Ponies to Hong Kong materialized quickly, and the officials at the Hong Kong Equestrian Federation were receptive. The ASPC purchased two very nice Shetland riding ponies. One of the ponies was the National Champion riding and driving pony FMF Imagination. Along with being a registered American Shetland Pony, Imagination's brown-and-white spotted coloring qualified him for dual registration with the Pinto Horse Association of America, an organization that accepts spotted equines from a wide variety of breeds. The second American Shetland Pony donated was PC's Karmel Kid, who was trained in the Olympic discipline of dressage.

The two Shetland show ponies flew from Chicago to Hong Kong on June 6, 2008. The Hong Kong Equestrian Federation hosted a televised media presentation ceremony on July 10, 2008, in Hong Kong to receive the ponies. After

Zona Schnieder presents PC Karmel Kid and FMF ➤ Imagination to the Hong Kong representatives.

the ceremony, the two Shetland Ponies were placed at two Hong Kong riding schools. They have been active in those school's programs ever since.

The two Shetland Ponies garnered a great deal of national and international media attention, and the story about the Shetland Ponies continues to attract attention on the Internet.

In the United States, the ASPC continues to keep Shetlands and Miniatures in the spotlight. Just six months after delivering the Shetland Ponies to Hong Kong, the ASPC donated a pony to the Arabian Nights Dinner Theater in Orlando, Florida. Tap Dance Kidd (Dancer), a three-time Grand National Champion American Shetland Pony, joined more than sixty other horses in the Arabian

PHOTO COURTESY OF Arabian Nights

⋏ Tap Dance Kidd dances through the lollipops at the Arabian Nights show in Orlando, Florida. The ASPC/AMHR donated the Shetland Pony to the dinner theater attraction.

PHOTO BY Johnny Robb

⚲ Tap Dance Kidd at his arrival ceremony at Arabian Nights in Orlando, Florida.

Nights cast to became the first-ever ambassador of the Shetland Pony breed to appear at the popular attraction.

"We were really excited to get a Shetland Pony for Arabian Nights," said Audrey Padgett, vice president of public relations and marketing for Arabian Nights. "We like to showcase different breeds and their variety of talents. Dancer is our fifteenth different breed in our show."

Staged in an enormous equestrian indoor-theater arena, Arabian Nights features fifty-nine horse stars and one Shetland Pony performer. The multi-breed cast of horses wears costumes and even gets makeup—all of which Dancer seems to love! More than a thousand visitors attend the dinner theater each

PHOTO COURTESY OF ASPC/AMHR and its members

⋏ PC Karmel Kid and FMF Imagination.

day, 365 days a year, which gives Shetland star Dancer a large audience to strut his stuff for!

The Arabian Nights Dinner Theater is also home to the Black Stallion Literacy Foundation. The Black Stallion Literacy Foundation has helped motivate hundreds of thousands of children to enjoy reading by connecting the magic of

Photo by Darcia Korvarik

Little Black shows off his performance skills for the Black Stallion Literacy Foundation. Bruce Becker of Brushcreek Shetlands, the 2008 Modern Shetland Pony Breeder of the Year, donated Little Black to the foundation.

live horses with reading. The Foundation, named after *The Black Stallion* books by Walter Farley, was cofounded in 1999 by Mark Miller, owner of Arabian Nights Dinner Attraction and Walter Farley's son, Tim Farley, with the idea that Arabian Nights and the Black Stallion could inspire children to stay interested in reading and lead more successful lives.

The 2008 Modern Shetland Pony Breeder of the Year, Bruce Becker of Brushcreek Shetlands, donated a black Shetland Pony who closely resembles the pony Little Black in the Walter Farley book *Little Black, a Pony* to the foundation. Brushcreek's Success, now known as Little Black, visits young students at their schools to promote reading.

PHOTO BY Johnny Robb

Through the Literacy Foundation, first graders are given the book *Little Black, a Pony* when their school takes part in the program. The trainers from Arabian Nights then take the two horses from the book, Little Black and Big Red, to the school so the children can have an up-close and personal experience with the horses they are reading about. There is little doubt that the children in the reading program will ever forget meeting the Little Black pony character in the flesh. For many children, the program fosters a love of reading and ponies that will last a lifetime!

# A PAIR OF MINIATURE HORSES EVERYONE CAN OWN

No matter where you live or what your lifestyle is, there are at least two Miniature Horses that are suitable for anyone to own. They are Breyer Miniature Horse Models Magic Man's Grand Slam and LTD's Red Cloud. Lisa Davis, owner of the real-life Grand Slam and Red Cloud, was flattered and excited when Breyer Animal Creations e-mailed her, requesting photos of her Miniature Horses for a possible Breyer model creation they were considering. "They were in the decision-making process for several months. I anxiously awaited their call to tell me if they were going to use one of my horses. When the phone call finally came, I was stunned! They had decided they weren't going to do just one of my horses, they were going to do two and make them a set. I was ecstatic, to say the least," said Lisa.

Breyer decided to immortalize Lisa's champion Miniature Horses in their Breeds of the World collection. Breyer couldn't have selected two better candidates to represent the breed. Between the two horses, they have amassed over thirty National Championship titles and literally hundreds of wins at shows

◄ Little Black poses with representatives from the Black Stallion Literacy Foundation.

PHOTO BY Washburn Photography

⋏ Magic Man's Grand Slam and LTD's Red Cloud go down in history as Breyer Miniature Horses.

nationwide, in both halter and performance classes. "I am really proud of them," Lisa said. "We breed, raise, train, and show our horses ourselves."

Lisa was especially pleased that Breyer selected Red Cloud, because despite

PHOTO BY Washburn Photography

becoming one of the most decorated champions in Lisa's stable, he had a rather shaky start. "Red Cloud started out as a very sickly foal. He was raised as a bottle baby in our basement. He grew up frolicking in the yard with our two Dobermans. He went on to win many national titles. He holds the record for winning the most Multi-Color Stallion awards in Miniature Horse history," Lisa recalls.

⋏ Red Cloud shows why he was selected as a Breyer model.

PHOTO BY Washburn Photography

⋏ Grand Slam and Red Cloud show off their Breyer statues.

When Red Cloud was selected as a Breyer model in 2006 he had been out of the show ring for six years. "I decided to take him back one more time in 2006, since he was honored as a Breyer Model. He once again won National Champion Multi-Color," said Lisa.

The Breyer Miniature Horse models became an instant success. Lisa and the horses were invited to attend Breyer Fest 2006. "We had a wonderful time showing off Grand Slam and Red Cloud. We participated in the model signings for the public, and the Miniatures themselves were a huge hit. Their models sold out at Breyer Fest, and we did a driving and jumping performance in front of over eight thousand people," Lisa shared.

PHOTO BY Washburn Photography

⋏ Magic Man's Grand Slam, a Breyer model, shows he is more than just a pretty face.

The Breyer Miniature Horses set continues to be very popular. Lisa donated one of the two original Breyer sets of her horses to the American Miniature Horse Registry's fundraising Trainer's Auction, and it sold for $1,100. Best of all, as Miniature Horse models, Grand Slam and Red Cloud are spreading the love of Miniature Horses in homes all over the globe.

## THE VERSATILITY OF THE SMALL EQUINE

"What exactly can you do with Shetlands and Miniatures?" The answer is simple: "Almost anything!" What the tiny equines lack in size they certainly make up for in ability. While Shetlands and Miniatures are favorites in the show ring, they can also be found excelling in combined driving events, trail rides, parades, pony rides, harness racing, 4-H projects, fox hunting, dressage

PHOTO BY Michael Bradtke

Photo courtesy of Isabel J. Kurek

⋏ A small equine and rider in pink show the crowd that they are small but mighty.

competitions, Pony Club, educational exhibits, and as gymkhana mounts and therapy equines. They are popular for lesson ponies and 4-H projects. And that list just scratches the surface.

The small equine's role as a healer and soother of the soul continues to expand as the number of equine therapy programs around the country grows. In addition, many owners of small equines arrange informal visits with their horses to schools and facilities in their own hometowns. Miniature Horses and small Shetlands are the perfect size to visit nursing homes, hospitals, and rehabilitation centers. Small equine service horses seem to have a sixth sense on how to

≺ A future pony hunter navigates a jump.

PHOTO COURTESY OF Matis Associates and Rod and Heather Hart

⚊ The Canadian Royal Mounted Police meets an eight-horse-hitch of small equines.

⚊ A team of small equines enjoys a snowy adventure.

PHOTO COURTESY OF THE ASPC/AMHR and its members

quietly raise the spirits of those who need it most. They are easy to travel with, and many therapy horses travel by minivan. Despite their tiny size, these equine healers deliver a vast amount of joy, hope, and comfort on every outing.

And while small equine therapy horses are doing their part to help and heal, small equines are bringing smiles to people in a variety of other expected and unexpected ways. With just a little investigating, it becomes apparent that the versatility of small equines is endless. Thanks to the people who love them, Shetland Ponies and Miniature Horses can be found in all walks of life, doing all sorts of jobs. In addition to being smart and quick learners, Shetland Ponies and Miniature Horses will always top the versatility list as a loving friend and perfect pint-size companion.

PHOTO COURTESY OF High Hopes Therapeutic Riding, Inc.

⚞ A Miniature Horse from High Hopes Therapeutic Riding, Inc. in Old Lyme, Connecticut, meets a new friend.

## Regency Performance Miniatures: A Driving Force

Horses have always been a passion for Jaye Ventresca of Regency Performance Miniatures in Pennsylvania. Jaye jokes that she started riding big horses when she was only three years old, and the size of her horses has been shrinking ever since.

Jaye strongly believes in the joy of driving Miniature Horses and regularly competes in pleasure driving shows and combined driving events. She loves to promote driving Miniatures by offering clinics and demonstrations, and she even uses her farm's Web site as an education tool for anyone interested in driving Miniature Horses.

"I worked for a Shetland breeding farm, Candage Pony Farm, in New York as a teenager and learned how to drive and how to train ponies to drive. As an adult I trained and drove other types of ponies. After raising a family, I wanted to start driving more and was interested in driving pairs. I saw an article about Miniature Horses in a local horse newspaper and decided to find out more," Jaye said, describing the beginning of her Miniature Horse adventure. "My

PHOTO COURTESY OF Regency Performance Miniatures

PHOTO COURTESY OF Regency Performance Miniatures

⋏ Regency Performance Miniatures prove they can perform.

husband and kids aren't as interested in Miniature Horses, but I find I have a 'special' family that has come together because of our love of horses. Kids and adults come to visit and stay to learn more about these wonderful animals."

Jaye's training and showing partner Margaret Henry found Jaye when she was looking for a companion for one of her horses a few years ago. "There are opportunities to compete at American Driving Society shows and events, and we like to do that type of competition," Jaye said. "I have driven Margaret's Kamelot's Remington Steel up to the Intermediate level at CDEs. He loves to do flying lead changes as he gallops through the cones courses."

⋋ Jaye Ventresca's Regency Performance Miniatures compete in pleasure driving shows and combined driving events.

Jaye's Miniature Horse Echo Falls Rhett's Socks looks a lot like Steel, so Jaye and Margaret decided to see if Socks and Steel could work as a pair. "They like each other and go well together. As a pair they have competed at Gladstone CDE twice, placing second both times. We also competed at Shoulderbone CDE, where they won."

While Socks has an outstanding show record—he won the Superior Achievement Award in 2008 from the New Jersey Equine Council—he is versatile and equally able to take part in activities such as heading to the local library with Jaye for Theme Day. "I took Socks and Echo Falls Apollo's Brett, and they were hugged by more than a thousand children over a five-hour period," Jaye said.

While Jaye truly loves her Miniature Horses—she no longer has full-size horses, and her stalls have been revamped to mini size—she also loves the people she meets along the way. From the people who visit her farm or Web site to the Miniature Horse lovers she meets at shows, they all bond over small equines— which is easy to do thanks to the pint-size packages of love and perfection.

## Pony Power in a Perfect Package: Peter and Kirstin

Lots of little girls dream about having a beautiful snow-white pony to call their own—a pony that nickers and comes running when called, a pony that is undeniably a best friend.

Ten-year-old Kirstin Sudbeck of Minnesota is living that dream, thanks to her American Shetland Pony named Teddyson's Easter Son, known as Peter. Together the pony and rider are a small but dynamic duo—pony power in a perfect package.

Kirstin's family bought Peter from Rosvold Farms, where Peter had been lightly started. The rest was up to Kirstin, who fell in love with her pony. They bonded, and the two are now best friends. "They are inseparable, and both would be miserable without the other," said Kirstin's mom, Heidi. "Peter trusts her more than anyone, and she trusts him just the same."

PHOTO COURTESY OF THE Sudbeck Family

⅄ Kirstin Sudbeck and her barrel racing buddy Peter—pony power in a perfect package.

At forty-one inches tall, Peter is always the smallest pony wherever the duo goes. Everyone who knows Shetland Ponies knows they are small but mighty, so being small doesn't bother Peter. "He outruns some of the bigger Quarter Horses," Kirstin said, laughing. "Also, Peter does not like to be last and is not afraid of anything. If we are out riding and my mom's big horse is scared of something, Peter will go first and check it out. Nothing bothers him."

Kirstin shows Peter in Western Pleasure classes, gaming events, and bareback classes, where he stays busy winning ribbons and trophies. "We have so much fun together, and I can ride him in a halter and lead rope. I trained him, and it was worth all the hard work," Kirstin said about her pony companion.

⋏ Kirstin Sudbeck and Peter race toward the finish line.

Kirstin's mom admires her pint-size daughter and calls her a one-of-a-kind pony lover who lives and breathes ponies and riding. "Peter was not always easy-going. He would try to pull a few fast ones on Kirstin, and she would just get back on and keep working. Now he is the type of pony anybody can get on and ride. Kirstin put a lot of work into him and is so proud of him. We have had so many people offer us thousands of dollars for Peter, but money can't buy you happiness. He is priceless in our eyes. He has taught our daughter more than just how to ride; he has taught her responsibility and what it means to truly love something and have that love returned to you."

## 4-H and Elk Hunting for Miniature Horses in the Wilds of Wyoming

While many families love their Miniature Horses because they are small and don't require lots of land, Ned and Jeannie Dunn love having their Miniature Horses in the wide-open spaces of Northwest Wyoming.

Ned and Jeannie operate Powell Valley Miniature Horses, forty miles from Yellowstone National Park, where the pure, clean air and open spaces of Wyoming provide the perfect backdrop for raising and training Minis. "For

⋎ Shetlands and Miniatures usually hold a special spot in the family.

PHOTO BY Darcia Korvarik

the past six years I have leased eighteen Miniature Horses to the Little Hooves 4-H Club. The Minis are driven, and each child has the same horse year after year, so the connection between the kids and horses is amazing," Jeannie said, adding that the program is a result of a state and community effort. "A grant was secured through the State of Wyoming 4-H program, and local fund-raisers, and Walmart helped purchase the harness and carts."

The 4-H Club drives Jeannie's Miniature Horses in parades and partici-pates in local competitions. "The Minis stay at my house, and the kids come to practice two or three times a week. In the summer I haul the horses to the fairgrounds quite often for practice. I teach driving and am working with another parent to help with all the hitching."

When Jeannie isn't working with the 4-H Club, she and Ned set out on a different kind of adventure—one that still involves their Miniature Horses. "My husband and I take the Minis elk hunting. It works quite well, as we pack all of our gear in the basket behind the cart seat," Jeannie said.

Jeannie recalls one elk-hunting adventure that turned out to be a little too adventurous. "We started out on what was a really beautiful day, but it became four feet of snow almost overnight," she said. "We started hearing wolves and had to keep the Minis in the horse trailer. The wolves came in sight about seventy-five feet from us. There were five of them, and they were almost as big as the horses."

Jeannie said their elk-hunting experiences continued later with great success, but that particular adrenaline-filled trip will always be remembered.

## Sharing a Little Love: 4-H Member Wins Miniature Colt

Tara Smith, an Ohio-based 4-H member, had her dreams come true in a big way when she was chosen as the lucky recipient of a Miniature colt. Harold and Thomas Graham, of Graham's Pony Farm in Mt. Vernon, Ohio, gave the Miniature Horse to Tara.

⅄ 4-H member Tara Smith's dreams came true when she won a Miniature Horse.

The Grahams donated the colt to the 4-H member to encourage youth participation in AMHR/ASPC activities. "We hope to encourage other large breeders across the country to offer a similar program with the 4-H in their area," said Tom, adding that he hopes the opportunities he gives to 4-H members will continue to nurture their interest in small equines into adulthood and also encourage other youth. "It's the youth members who will carry the registry forward. They are our future."

The Grahams made the offer to all Lorain County 4-H youths who submitted an essay describing their needs and why they would be a good horse owner. In addition to the essay, the winner had to be able to provide adequate stabling and be able to meet financial costs associated with keeping a small equine. Applicants also had to submit two letters of recommendation and agree to join ASPC/AMHR and show the colt in a recognized show.

No doubt this little horse will be the start of something big! "He is a dream come true," Tara said.

## Tiny Dreams Come True at Caribbean Dreams Miniatures

More than twenty years ago, Linda Kern of Caribbean Dreams Miniatures in Loxahatchee, Florida, had no idea she would become an ambassador for the Miniature Horse breed when she bought a grade Shetland Pony for $50 and four beers. "That started us on a track that we had no clue would lead us to where we are today," Linda said with a laugh. "The family we bought Patchy from had boats and dogs but knew nothing about horses."

PHOTO BY Aurora Boyington

⋏ Linda Kerns of Caribbean Dreams Miniatures competes her four-in-hand Miniature team, while a team of Friesian four-in-hand follows behind.

Linda took a crash course in ponies, only to discover she loved them. Soon she was driving Patchy in a beach cart that had been used on the boardwalk in Ocean Beach, Maryland. "Our trainer suggested that we contact the American Miniature Horse Registry because Patchy was so small, so we did. The AMHR was extremely helpful, and Patchy became Lil' Miss Patches, a registered Miniature Horse," Linda said. "By the way, twenty-two years later we still have Patchy and the beach cart. Both have taught many children and adults to drive and experience the wonderful world of Miniature Horses, along with developing the skills needed to compete in local and national shows, as well as parades and other fun events."

◁ Linda Kerns takes one of her Miniature Horses out for a Sunday drive.

Over the years, Linda's family moved ten times with the Coast Guard before landing in Florida. "Each time we moved it involved more Minis, carts, dogs, cats, and even fish and hermit crabs," Linda said. "But all along the way the most important thing was being an ambassador for the breed and showing what Miniature Horses are capable of—which is anything and everything."

Linda believes Miniature Horses can do it all, whether in competition or just driving down the road. "We have done parades in California, Pennsylvania, Virginia, and Florida. We have taken horses to daycares, kindergartens, and private schools. Lil' Miss Patches was the Southernmost Reindeer in Key West, bringing Santa Claus from the Coast Guard boat to the Audubon House and Tropical Gardens. She was also the One-Horse Open Sleigh at the Space Coast Philharmonic in Cocoa Beach, where she trotted twice around the stage with the whole orchestra in the back before picking up the conductor on the third round and trotting out of the auditorium," Linda said, adding that her Minis have also taken part in a multitude of weddings and birthday parties over the

PHOTO BY Ken Braddick

◄ Combined Driving champion Chester Weber, who competes full-size equines internationally, takes a smaller four-in-hand, owned by Caribbean Dreams Miniatures, for a spin, with help from Timmy Dutta.

◄ Boones Little Buckeroo shows off his magnificent presence.

years. "Weddings are fun when the horses learn that wedding cake is almost as good as carrots. I can't forget to mention birthday parties—birthday cake is just as good as wedding cake."

Proving that Minis are a versatile breed, Linda also competes in driving events, such as singles, pairs, in tandem, unicorns, and four-in-hand. She recently bought a chariot and is configuring it to be able to drive four abreast. "Caribbean Dreams Miniatures has competed in many different classes over the years, in everything from hunter to showmanship and from halter to obstacle classes. These small wonders have shown in American Miniature Horse Registry, American Miniature Horse Association, and American Driving Society events," Linda said. "Every venue offers new and exciting challenges and opportunities! These organizations go above and beyond to offer the widest range of events, clinics, and camaraderie to their members. They are each phenomenal, and we wouldn't be the breed we are if it weren't for all the hard work and vision that each of these venues offer."

## A Miniature Horse Named Mr. Ed is Easy to Spot

Many horse fans are familiar with the theme song to the old television show *Mr. Ed*, but a little girl in Wyoming sings the song a little differently: "A horse is a horse, of course of course, and no one can talk to a horse, of course. That is, of course, unless that horse is a Miniature Horse named Mr. Ed."

Five-year-old Maggie McStay is the proud owner of a leopard Appaloosa Miniature Horse whose registered name is Shelly-Ann's First Edition, but like the famous talking horse, the spotted Mini goes by the name of Mr. Ed. While Maggie is head-over-heels in love with Mr. Ed, it seems the love affair goes both ways. "When Maggie goes outside and Mr. Ed can see her, he immediately goes to the fence and vies for her attention," said Maggie's mom, Heidi McStay. "If Maggie is playing with the dogs or doing something else, Mr. Ed will weave at the fence, paw, whinny, and do whatever it takes to capture her attention."

◄ Even in the
mountains,
Mr. Ed and
Maggie
are easy to
spot.

Love doesn't get much ➤
better than this, as
Maggie gives
Mr. Ed a hug.

⋏ Maggie and Mr. Ed pause for a snack and an amazing view.

Maggie and Mr. Ed are constant companions, whether they are playing in Maggie's playhouse or taking a pack trip up into the mountains. Maggie's mom laughs when she describes the pair's devotion to each other. "In Wyoming the winters go on forever and are relentlessly cold and windy, so sometimes you have to be creative when it comes to keeping your children entertained. I just bring Mr. Ed into our kitchen, and Maggie will spend hours brushing him and riding him around the kitchen. Our floors are stone so it works out great."

Having their Miniature Horse hang out in the kitchen isn't the only time Mr. Ed ventures into the house. One time Heidi and Maggie were unloading groceries, and when they weren't looking Mr. Ed sneaked into the kitchen and helped himself to some of the family's groceries, including a new bag of apples, which he tasted before scattering slobbery bits and chunks of apples throughout the kitchen.

"We leased Mr. Ed for the first year we had him because so many people warned me that ponies could be miserable. Boy, is that far from the truth! Mr. Ed is a cross between a dog, horse, and human. He is Maggie's best friend, and more often than not he fills in as her babysitter or the sibling that she doesn't have. He is so intelligent and kind," Heidi said.

Like his famous talking namesake, the little Mr. Ed is quite willing to be pampered in the barn, in a field, or even in the master bathroom of the house. Heidi laughs when she tells the story of the time she and Maggie had to take Mr. Ed into the wall-to-wall stone shower in her bathroom because he needed a bath—but it was 10 degrees below zero outside.

"Mr. Ed had developed an allergic reaction to some mineral oil product I had put in his mane and had lost his hair on his neck in the areas that the

⋎ A furry coat and a furry hat keep Mr. Ed and Maggie warm.

PHOTO COURTESY OF THE McStay Family

ʌ Maggie and Mr. Ed on a ride with mom Heidi in the Twilight Basin.

mineral oil had touched him," Heidi recalls. "The vet advised we bathe him to remove the oil from his neck, but it was too cold outside so we brought Mr. Ed into my bathroom. He fit perfectly in the shower."

Heidi said Mr. Ed thoroughly enjoyed his Mini Day Spa in the shower before being led to the laundry room, where they burned up two hair dryers trying to dry his wooly winter coat. "We were only able to get him about 90 percent dry, and I was worried about taking him outside because it was supposed to be well below 20 degrees that night. So we made a hay bed for him in the garage and brought in his pygmy goat friend to keep him company. The next morning when I walked into the garage, I couldn't stop laughing. The hay beds we made for the pony and goat to sleep in were untouched, and those two little hooligans were curled up on our dog's elevated dog beds as snug as bugs in a rug—and my dogs were looking at me from their perch on top of the four-wheeler as if to say, 'Get these freeloaders out of our garage!'"

Heidi added to the shower story by saying that while giving Mr. Ed a shower, she encouraged Maggie not to tell her daddy that their bathroom had been turned into a Mini spa, because they were trying to sell the house and a pony in the shower wasn't a great selling point. Maggie promised, but the

▾ Buckeye WCF Classical Blue Eyed Baby shows off her baby blues.

PHOTO BY Getitia Matheny

second her dad Kurtis walked in the door that night, she ran into the kitchen and as fast as she could talk said, "Daddy, Daddy, Daddy, Mr. Ed took a shower in your shower today, and Mommy blew him dry and now he's in the garage with the goat."

The look on Maggie's face was so priceless that Kurtis didn't mind—and in fact, the story helped sell their house. "It turned out the people who bought our home love animals as much as I do, and the story about a Mini taking a shower in the master bathroom is what sealed the deal on the sale of our home," Heidi said.

While Mr. Ed has had plenty of indoor experiences with Maggie, he and his little rider have also spent plenty of time exploring the great outdoors of Wyoming. "Mr. Ed is the best thing that has ever happened to us," Heidi said,

⅄ The world would be a better place if every child had a pony like Mr. Ed.

PHOTO COURTESY OF THE McStay Family

adding that when they head out on their pack trips, sheep hunting trips, and trail riding adventures, Maggie and Mr. Ed are decked out in a pink pony poncho with a Strawberry Shortcake canteen dangling over the saddle horn. "We look more like a circus act than a hunting party."

Mr. Ed and Maggie have earned quite a following in their state, and people often talk about the little girl seen riding high up in the mountains on the tiny spotted horse. That's all fine with the Miniature Horse named Mr. Ed, who is almost as famous—especially in Wyoming—as the talking horse from the television show.

## A Dozen Doers: Arizona's Miniature Drill Team

Visitors of the New Year's Day Rose Bowl Parade in Pasadena, California, are always thrilled by the small drill team that takes part in the giant parade—a team made up of a twelve-member Miniature Horse driving drill team known as the AZ Mini Mystique.

PHOTO COURTESY OF THE AZ Mini Mystique

◁ The AZ Mini Mystique Drill Team in perfect formation.

The Arizona team, led by Ron and JoAnne Souza, specializes in entertaining the public with an exciting and unique precision drill set to lively music. "Parades are a specialty of the AZ Mini Mystique," JoAnne said, adding that the team has been performing together for several years and has proudly represented the Miniature Horse at prestigious events such as the Rose Bowl Parade, the Del Mar National Horse Show, the Lost Dutchman Parade, and the Fiesta Bowl Parade.

The AZ Mini Mystique doesn't just perform in parades but is also active in community service. Many of the team members take their Miniature Horses to hospitals, assisted-living centers, schools, libraries, and therapeutic riding centers. "The AZ Mini Mystique is also dedicated to educating the public about the Miniature Horse," JoAnne said, adding that they actively support Miniature Horse rescue and the prevention of equine cruelty, offering foster homes for abused and abandoned Miniature Horses.

## Three-Ring Circus

For Lisa Dufresne of Sarasota, Florida, performing with her Miniature Horses really is a three-ring circus. Her troop of eight Miniature Horses delights audiences wherever they go. Lisa, an accomplished Grand Prix dressage rider, purchased a trick horse that lead her on a path that would include a two-year stint performing at Arabian Nights, followed by twelve years on the road with the Ringling Brothers Circus, including three years performing in Japan. Earlier in her career she worked with eight full-size Quarter Horses in a liberty act, followed by more exotic liberty acts including zebras, llamas, camels, and even pigs!

When she returned to the University of Florida to complete her degree in 1996, Lisa decided to downsize her act and purchased six matched Miniature stallions. "I absolutely fell in love with them," said Lisa. "They were so easy

Lisa Dufresne and one of her Miniature Horses performs in the show "Horses, Horses, Horses." ➤

to train, and some of them were not even halter broke when I got them." Like many big-horse converts, Lisa admits she had to remember they were horses, not pets, and that her troop was all stallions. "I really had to resist the temptation to spoil them. They are still horses and need to be treated like horses," added Lisa.

PHOTO COURTESY OF Lisa Dufresne

PHOTO COURTESY OF Lisa Dufresne

⋏ Lisa Dufresne gets her Miniatures in order.

Before long, Lisa took her six-horse Miniature Liberty act on the road, and the crowds loved them. Lisa's six stallions, Hans, Reo, Rex, Jasper, Duke, and Pipsqueak, were soon joined by two more Miniatures, Vita and Stormy. Lisa trained Vita and Stormy to do a trick act, and soon they were a favorite part of her show.

Today, Lisa and her Miniature Horse act, called "Horses, Horses, Horses," charm audiences at fairs, circuses, and shows around the country. Lisa says her Miniatures "are like a bunch of kids. They are just so entertaining." Her delighted audiences couldn't agree more!

◁ Miniature Horses love to perform.

⅄ Six Miniature Horses delight the crowd during their act.

## Chariot Racing Drives Bryant's Miniatures

Hal and Deb Bryant may look like regular Miniature Horse owners, until they hitch their black-and-white Minis to chariots and turn into Ben-Hur look-a-likes. "We have all watched Ben-Hur and the Roman chariot races," Hal said. "It is thrilling to watch, and it may look easy to do, but chariot driving is probably the most difficult driving discipline there is to do properly and safely with a team of Miniature Horses."

Hal and Deb Bryant enjoy life as Ben-Hur look-a-likes. ➢

PHOTO COURTESY OF Bryant's Miniatures

PHOTO BY Washburn Photography

ᐱ Hal and Deb Bryant and their famous black-and-white Miniature Horses.

The Bryants own Bryant's Miniatures in Illinois, where they not only participate in chariot races but also raise, train, and show Miniatures. "Our breeding program of thirty years has produced a tradition of black-and-white Miniature Horses with exceptional bloodlines suited to the athletic ability needed to be a top hitch horse," Hal said. "We train year-round, which includes sleigh riding in the winter months!"

The high speeds and tight turns of chariot racing makes it a tricky sport, and Hal said perfect balance is a must in chariot racing. "If you stand too far back, the pole comes up and can lift the front feet of your team off the ground. If you stand too far forward, you are putting weight on their necks and pushing their feet into the ground," Hal said.

Chariot driving is the only class that requires the horses to gallop or canter at top speed. If both horses are in sync, it is an exciting ride. If they are not, it takes a good driver and an even better team to control the situation. "For all the concerns to consider when driving chariots, we truly enjoy the rush we get from the demonstrations we do at many events. We have matching chariots and love to compete!" Hal said.

Bryant's Miniatures show off their chariot skills and their black-and-white Miniature Horses.

PHOTO BY Washburn Photography

# Small Equines Shine
# in the Show Ring

Shetland Ponies and Miniature Horses really seem to love being the center of attention and really turn on their charm in the show ring. Sanctioned Miniature Horse and Shetland shows are held throughout the United States, including eight National Area shows hosted in each region of the country. There are also two National Championship shows hosted each year. The Shetland Pony Congress is hosted each year in a central location, usually in the center of the country, in late July and early August. The AMHR Miniature Horse Nationals are held annually each September in Tulsa, Oklahoma.

PHOTO BY Johnny Johnston

⋏ Falling in love with a Miniature Horse is easy.

The AMHR National Championship Show is a ten-day extravaganza for Miniature Horse competitors. Typically over fifteen hundred converge on Tulsa, and the show often has well over five thousand entries, making it one of the largest all-breed shows in the country.

The AMHR National Championship Show offers three hundred classes for Miniature Horses to enter. Competitions in halter, driving, jumping, costume, youth classes, and more stir the crowd as they cheer on their favorites. And with over $50,000 in cash and prizes in championship and futurity classes, the atmosphere is one of high stakes and high spirits. The nation's top professional, amateur, and youth competitors compete for top honors. Despite some

⅄ Miniature Perfection: Martha Hickham and trainer Ray Zoercher pose with El Rancho Loco.

PHOTO BY Liz McMillan

PHOTO COURTESY OF ASPC/AMHR and its members

◄ The Miniature Horse is so adorable they have fans of all ages.

very large classes with fifty or more entries, only one horse will take home the coveted title of National Champion in each class.

AMHR Miniature Horses may compete in one of two divisions: Division "A" Miniatures must stand at thirty-four inches and under, while Division "B" Miniatures must measure under thirty-eight inches. Unlike Shetland Ponies and full-size horses, a Miniature Horse's height is measured at the last hair at the bottom of their mane to the ground. Prior to showing, all Miniature

Little Kings Buck by Buck and Boones Little Buckeroo take a moment to say hello. ➤

Horses must be measured by the show officials. There are numerous halter classes for each Miniature height division.

Horses are judged on their conformation and movement. In addition, the halter horses are separated by age and gender, so that the judges are comparing horses of similar heights, genders, and ages. Some classes are judged strictly on

PHOTO BY Washburn Photography

◄ Handler and horse keep their eyes on the judge.

PHOTO BY Stuart Vesty

color and showmanship, and some classes are judged on the handler's skills. Classes are further divided into open, amateur, and youth divisions. The youth divisions are divided into three age categories. Despite the many divisions, the halter classes at the AMHR Nationals are very large, and the competition often runs well into the night as the three judges select their top ten places.

The Liberty class is a favorite of both the spectators and the horses themselves. As the name suggests, the individual horses are set free in the arena to show off their movement and beauty at liberty. They perform to music selected by their handlers. When the music stops, the handler has one minute to catch the horse—a task that can be entertainment unto itself. As a rule, friendly Miniature show horses are very easy to catch and often run to their handlers after the music ends, but sometimes the excitement of being free in the show rings gets the best off them and there is no stopping the show! If the horse is not caught and haltered in the prescribed time, the entry is eliminated. It is a beautiful and exciting class, and the crowds cheer for their favorites.

For those who are eager to show off their horse's performance skills, there are a number of driving classes for everything from speedy roadster classes, where the drivers are dressed in racing silks and are seated in sulkies, to elegant park turnout driving classes. There are multiple hitch classes, park horse driving classes, country pleasure driving classes, obstacle driving classes, and even chariot driving classes, where drivers turn out in Roman togas. Like the halter divisions, the numerous driving classes are divided for amateur, youth, and men and ladies.

There are a number of other performance classes, including both hunter and jumper over fences classes. The one big difference in Miniature Horse jumping is that the handler runs alongside the horse while it jumps the course, rather than riding it over the fences. The jump courses look similar to big horse courses, and the course pattern is posted prior to the event. As with full-size jumpers, jump-offs are speed events, which mean the handlers have to keep up with their speedy jumpers to take the prize.

Versatility is a very popular class that combines halter, jumping, and driving. Each horse is presented and judged in hand, then shown over a combination of jumps, and then hitched up and shown as a driving horse. The horse never leaves the ring, and a handler can assist the competitor with tack changes. To win this class, the Miniature has to have very good conformation and excellent performance training.

⋎ Personality plus. A Miniature Horse shows off at the trot.

PHOTO BY Johnny Johnston

Creative ➢ costumes are a winning combination.

PHOTO BY Washburn Photography

Because of the horses' very small stature, the only official riding class at the AMHR Nationals is the Children's Leadline Class. While the riders are under seven years old, they are turned out to perfection and relish the opportunity to show off their riding skills. On occasion you will see a mounted child in the Costume Class at the AMHR Nationals.

The Costume Class is one class that no spectator at the AMHR Nationals wants to miss. Here imaginations are left to run wild, and the spectators often do the same. Miniature Horses are transformed into planes, trains, aliens, cows, dogs, zebras, astronauts, elephants, hula dancers, candy bars, campfires, and more. There is no limit to the amount of sheer creativity and work that goes into these costumes. This very large class consistently fills the stands of the coliseum. There is truly no predicting what you'll see in the Miniature Horse Costume Class, but one thing is guaranteed—you will be amazed and entertained.

The AMHR Nationals also has a PMC division, with classes for physically or mentally challenged horse lovers of all ages in almost every division. Because of their size and friendly natures, Miniature Horses are often used to help build skills and confidence for children and adults with a variety of physical or mental challenges. There are few things more rewarding than sharing the glory as one of the shows many PMC competitors overcomes personal challenges to win a National Championship. Among the competitors and the spectators, there are truly no losers in these classes.

⋎ Pretty as a picture. A Miniature Horse strikes a pose.

PHOTO BY Washburn Photography

## Miniature Horse Ambassador, Johnathon Eckbold Knows What It Truly Means to Win

Johnathon Eckbold has overcome a lot in his twenty years. Born with spina bifida, Johnathon has endured thirty surgeries and continues to deal with medical issues. That hasn't stopped the New Jersey native from leading a full life—a life complete with Miniature Horses that help Johnathon thrive and enjoy every day to the fullest.

Johnathon's family owns Flying J Farm, home to his beloved Minis, Im A Buck Private and Mountain Meadows American Express. His passion for Minis started when Johnathon was young. A friend of his mom's invited them

⋎ Miniature Horse ambassador Johnathon Eckbold shows his Miniature Horse.

PHOTO BY Washburn Photography

PHOTO BY Washburn Photography

⋏ Johnathon Eckbold (center) and his proud family.

over to ride her Miniature Horse. It didn't take long before the Eckbold family was hooked on Minis.

"I show my Miniature Horses in halter, showmanship, liberty, obstacle driving, halter obstacle, hunter, and all disciplines of driving," Johnathon said. "Working with Minis has helped with my confidence and allowed me to be part of a great breed. Plus I have been able to represent the Miniature Horse by being an Ambassador for the American Miniature Horse Registry."

Johnathon's disability hasn't slowed him down, but it has served as an inspiration to others. "I try and encourage other people with disabilities to get out there and try new things," he said, adding that it hasn't always been an easy road. "My first Mini was named Kate, and she taught me so much. I was showing her in a hunter class once; we were coming to the last jump, and I tripped on a rock and let go of the line. She went over the jump without me and stood there waiting for me to get up."

Johnathon hopes to be a breeder and trainer someday, but in the meantime he is thankful for the friends he has met in the Miniature Horse world. "Showing Miniature Horses has allowed me to have great, long-term friendships," Johnathon said. "I look forward to going to the shows to hang out with my friends."

## YOUNGSTERS SHINE IN THE YOUTH DIVISION

The youth division classes at the AMHR Nationals mimic the adult divisions and are also highly competitive. The youth program at the AMHR Nationals involves teamwork and a variety of fun and educational events between classes that culminate with an exciting youth essay contest. In a very exciting ceremony, the youth essay winners are awarded a Miniature Horse.

⋎ Children of all ages can take part in driving, a big benefit of a small equine.

PHOTO BY Washburn Photography

washburn©

Because of the size ratio of horse to youth handler, children at the AMHR Nationals tend to be more hands-on preparing their horses for the show ring. It is not surprising to see children as young as five bathing, clipping, and working their horses in hand before competition. It is one of the unique advantages that small equines offer, and it develops confidence and self-esteem within the youth competitors.

A great deal of socializing, shopping, and even some horse trading also makes the AMHR Nationals more than just a horse show. At the end of the ten-day affair, it is always bittersweet for competitors to pack up and go home.

## Champion Becomes Big Fan of Small Equines

With multiple national titles to her credit, Janice Bryant is a familiar face at the AMHR Nationals year after year. But it didn't start out that way. Janice, who now owns Morningview Farms, a small Miniature Horse and Classic Foundation Shetland Pony breeding farm in Chattanooga, Tennessee, was not a fan of small equines. Like many big horse people, she wondered, "What use is a horse that you can't ride?"

That all changed when she went to a horse auction in 2000 to purchase tack and ended up rescuing a thirty-two-and-a-half-inch Miniature Horse instead. "Now we are passionate about performance and believe our small equines should be versatile enough to be useful as well as pretty," Janice said. "We breed athletic driving horses with wonderful color and great conformation. They have the ability to win national-level driving titles as well as national-level halter titles."

The little Miniature stallion that Janice rescued at the auction went on to win multiple National Top Ten Championships. "His first filly, MVF Take A Chance, earned National Top Ten honors as a yearling," Janice said proudly. "Then we branched out into the Over Division with Little Kings Patch The Buck in 2005. My daughter broke him to drive, and in three short years he earned five National Championships, three Reserve National Championships, and multiple top tens."

Janice said that Morningview Farms was so excited about raising, training, and showing Miniature Horses that they then branched into color classes with an Appaloosa stallion that they co-own with Amazing Sunrise Miniatures and Cathy Buehrer. Their enthusiasm over small equines didn't stop there. Janice said Morningview is now ready to experience the versatility of the Shetland

⋎ Janice Bryant, of Morningview Farms, enjoys showing and raising Miniature Horses so much that she wants every day to be a Mini day!

PHOTO BY Washburn Photography

PHOTO BY Getitia Matheny

⅄ Buckeye WCF Classical I Sizzle demonstrates his jumping skills at a very young age.

Pony. "We have taken the bull by the horns and now proudly own a Classic American Shetland Pony, a stunning thirty-five-and-a-quarter-inch yearling filly. We can't wait to start our Shetland adventure," Janice said.

Whether it's Shetland Ponies or Miniature Horses, Janice said she has opened her heart to the endearing and wonderful small equines. "These little guys enrich my life daily, and I can't ever imagine it not being a Mini day!"

# THE SHETLAND PONY NATIONAL CONGRESS

While Shetland Ponies are larger than their Miniature counterparts, the Shetland Pony National Congress is smaller than the AMHR Nationals. The show runs for five days and packs a lot of excitement into those five days and nights!

Like the AMHR National Championship Show, the Congress offers hundreds of classes, including halter, driving, jumping, costume, and amateur and youth divisions. The Shetland Pony National Congress also offers a number of riding classes for children and their ponies including leadline, equitation classes, jumping, and even barreling racing for young riders.

The Shetland Pony National Congress also offers hunter and jumper classes for adults and children that are conducted like the Miniature jumping classes, with the handler running beside the pony over the course.

Shetland halter and performance classes are also divided by age and gender. In addition, there are divisions for the Classic Shetlands, Foundation Shetlands, Modern Shetlands, American Show Ponies, and National Show Ponies.

A number of specialty classes include the ever-popular costume class, numerous driving classes, including the not-to-be-missed Fancy Turnout class, and futurity and stakes classes. In the Fancy Turnout class, elegant drivers are dressed to the nines in elaborate formal wear that is reminiscent of days gone by.

The Shetland Pony National Congress also hosts a Liberty class with the same rules as the Miniature Liberty classes. Many pony fans agree that the Modern Shetland Liberty class is one of the most exciting of the show. These electrifying ponies strut their stuff at liberty, and the fans go wild. They are truly breathtaking.

In 2008, the American Shetland Pony Club celebrated its 120th anniversary with a specially designed commemorative trophy for winners at the American Shetland Pony Congress. The sculptured pony on the commemorative trophy was designed by artist Nancy Belden and modeled after a primitive iron statue

PHOTO BY Johnny Johnston

◄ Small equines
are intelligent
and beautiful—a
wonderful
combination.

of the famed American Shetland Pony stallion, Frisco Pete, a six-time National Halter Champion stallion that has had a great influence on the breed.

The Shetland Pony National Congress also hosts an extensive array of youth events at the show, including educational games, scavenger hunts, youth judging contests, youth team events, as well as youth essay contests. The lucky winners of the essay contests take home a beautiful Shetland Pony, which is awarded in a moving ceremony hosted in the main arena.

PHOTO BY Johnny Johnston

◄ All the beauty and power of a large horse, packaged in a small body.

Similar to the AMHR Nationals, the Shetland Pony National Congress is also an annual event. Along with showing ponies, shopping, socializing, and pony trading are going on throughout the event amidst an air of excitement and opportunity.

## Showing in Style

Jim and Becky McKeith started their small-equine adventure on a whim—and that whim has taken them on a great adventure full of winning Miniature Horses and Shetland Ponies. "Neither of us had ever owned horses, and we learned everything ourselves," Becky said, recalling how they started with their first Miniature Horse in 1995.

Now the owners of Snowberry Farm Miniature Horses in Michigan, Becky looks back at their adventure with a great sense of humor. "I always wanted a horse, but my parents couldn't afford one," she said. "I saw a Miniature foal, and Jim made me promise not to buy it. Of course I did, and within the next few months we had five."

Their adventure with Miniatures turned out to be a success, so Jim and Becky then decided to enter the Shetland Pony world. "A friend needed a place to keep a Shetland Pony. He brought him to our farm, and that's how it all started," Becky said, adding that they now have Modern Shetlands and thoroughly enjoy the breed.

Jim and Becky's program has developed and grown over the years. They have produced several Modern Shetland champions, including Ken-Mar's Man, a Modern Shetland Pony that was the 2008 World and Congress Grand Champion, Modern Roadster, and Tams As Good As It Gets, another Modern Shetland that was named 2008 World and Congress Grand Champion Fine Harness, and 2007 Pony of the Year, Modern Performance.

PHOTO BY Johnny Johnston

Thanks to their ➤ stunning looks, small equines have become extremely popular.

PHOTO BY Washburn Photography

Becky McKeith of Snowberry Farm Miniature Horses, dressed in an evening gown and opera gloves, shows that driving can be a stylish experience.

Becky said she and Jim make a great team, but she does it with a bit more style—fashion style, that is. Becky, who says she loves everything about fashion, has set the standard in the Miniature Horse and Shetland Pony world when it comes to style. "I love to get dressed up and wear elaborate outfits," Becky said. "When I started driving I began to wear long, beaded gowns, and it is so much fun."

PHOTO BY Mason Photography

⋏ A beautiful chestnut foal.

# Acknowledgments

We extend our heartfelt thanks to the many small equine lovers throughout the country who shared their amazing stories and photos and to the professional photographers who contributed so many extraordinary photos. This book would not have been possible without your contributions. And a very special thanks to our celebrity contributors, bestselling mystery author and accomplished equestrian Tami Hoag and TV personality and lifelong horseman Carson Kressley. We know how busy you two are and are grateful you took time out to share your "small equine" tales with us! And a special thanks to the board and members of the American Shetland Pony Club and the American Miniature Horse Registry, your vision and support brought this book to its fruition. And thanks to Erin at the office, who had to put up with long hours and pitch in on so many aspects of the book. And Jackson and Abby, for their support as we worked!

# Appendix

## Photographers of the Small Equine

*A special thanks to all the photographers who contributed to this book. Without your beautiful images, this book could not have been produced.*

**Ken Bennison**

www.geocities.com/kenbenca/homepage.html

kenbennison@hotmail.com

Ken Bennison, along with his wife Maureen, owns and operates Snowy Acres Miniature Horses in Northern Ontario, Canada. Bennison has been an adventure photographer for many years. Now retired, he devotes more time to raising these wonderful little horses and photographing them as they go about their daily lives.

### Barbara Bower

www.equineartistrybybarbara.com

barbara@barbarasvisions.com

Barbara Bower has been a professional photographer for over thirty years. Combining her two passions of photography and animals is her greatest joy. Bower has earned her PPA and master's of photography and photographic craftsman degrees and has received the Accolade of Lifetime Photographic Excellence Award.

### Aurora Boyington

www.wellingtonphoto.com

auroramarie621@hotmail.com

Aurora Boyington is a second-generation photographer with thirty-two years of equestrian experience. Boyington has a vast amount of experience photographing equines from a variety of disciplines and breeds, including dressage, polo, steeplechase, hunter/jumper, and small equines. Boyington is also skilled with family portraits, wedding photography, and graduation photos, as well as Web site design.

### Ken Braddick

www.kenbraddick.com

ken@dressage-news.com

Ken Braddick has been deeply involved in the equestrian world for many years. Braddick recently launched dressage-news.com, a Web site created to provide dressage news, photo and video reports from around the world. He also created the glossy full-color magazine *HorseSport USA* that focuses on high-performance dressage and jumping.

**Michael F. Bradtke**

386-795-3863

www.michaelbradtkephotography.com

Since acquiring his first 35 mm camera at the age of fifteen, Michael Bradtke has demonstrated a gift. Bradtke's vision navigates us through thought, feeling, and emotion. A familiar face at horse shows, Michael is available by appointment for private and public functions.

**Bob Brown**

Unicorner Photography

254-749-2332

rdbrown@unicornerfarm.com

Bob Brown is located near Waco, Texas. He has been raising Miniature Horses for over fourteen years at his Unicorner Farm. Brown has an excellent understanding of horses that translates in his photography.

**Robin Cole**

813-431-7576

flaminihorseclub@aol.com

Robin Cole is deeply involved with small equines and is the secretary of the Florida Miniature Horse Club. Cole is a talented photographer. Her photographs have been widely published on the Web and in print.

**Cathy Franks Photography**

330-466-3365

foxlanefarm@yahoo.com

Cathy Franks studied photography at the Art Institute of Fort Lauderdale. With her husband, Franks raises, trains, and shows American Shetland Ponies and American Miniature Horses. Franks says, "I love the endeavor of capturing the true beauty of these incredible horses through the art of photography."

**Jodie French**

Foley, MN

llilones@aol.com

www.miniatureequine.com/jfrench

Jodie French has been a photographer for more than twenty years. French has a great deal of experience in the equine world as a participant and as a judge, giving her a wide knowledge base and understanding of the breed. She has specialized in small-equine photography for over five years.

**Simm Gottesman**

Boca Raton, FL

561-488-4887

acusimm@gmail.com

Simm Gottesman is a professional photographer and acupuncture physician. An avid philanthropist who has been involved with a wide array of charities and organizations, Simm said, "I love animals, especially Shetlands and Miniature Horses, and would jump at any opportunity to promote these little awesome creatures and their larger counterparts, the *big* horses."

**Rebekah Holt**

www.equest4truth.com

equest@neto.com

For many years, Rebekah Holt has been a great contributor of promotional photos of Shetland Ponies and Miniature Horses. Rebekah captures the spirit of small equines by photographing their interactions with children and each other.

**Barbara Johnson Photography**

320-224-2325

www.bjp.photoreflect.com

Barbara Johnson's photographic specialties include: adventure/extreme, children, church, event, nature/wildlife, parties and events, people/lifestyle, pets, portrait, and wedding.

**Johnny Johnston**

425-885-9660

photosbyjohnny@gmail.com

Johnny Johnston has become a legend in equine photography. Johnston has years of experience capturing beautiful images of top horses in the United States and around the world. His work contributed to revolutions in the field of equine photography. Johnston, based near Seattle, Washington, is highly sought-after for a variety of equine breeds.

**Darcia Korvarik**

308-942-3475

www.dkimage-design.com

www.miniatureequine.com/outlaw

darcia@myphotomax.com

Darcia Korvarik and her husband Ray own dk Designs & Photography. The couple also owns Outlaw Miniatures and Shetland Ponies and have been raising small equines for over twenty years. Korvarik said, "Each moment is a gift. We want to help you ensure that your memories last forever."

**Isabel J. Kurek**

301-943-32077

410-741-0999

isabelkurek@aol.com

Isabel Kurek's work has been widely published in magazines including *Maryland Life* magazine, *W* magazine, *The Equiery*, *The Chronicle of the Horse*, *In and Around Horse Country*, and many others.

**Bob Langrish**

+44 (0)1452 770140

bob@boblangrish.co.uk

Based in England, Bob Langrish has spent thirty-seven years specializing in equine photography. He has built an equestrian photographic library of over 400,000 pictures covering all aspects of the horse.

**Mason Photography**

Richard Mason

www.mason-photography.com

Located in the Hill Country of Texas between Austin and San Antonio, Mason Photography strives to provide the highest quality images that capture the imagination. Mason says, "My specialty is creative quality. My interests are many."

**Getitia Matheny**

Buckeye Walnut Creek Farm

(704) 474 3569

www.buckeyeWCF.com

buckeyewcf@aol.com

Getitia Matheny, along with husband Les, owns and operates Buckeye Walnut Creek Farm in central Ohio. The farm focuses on breeding small equines to have outstanding conformation and features. Getitia also has the ability to capture her equine creations in photos.

**Liz McMillan**

www.equineimagery.com

**Nelson Photography**

Michele Nelson

www.nelsonpics.com

nelson@nelsonpics.com

Mark and Michele Nelson are a professional couple who photograph horses, large and small. Nelson Photography is based in Oakland, California, and specializes in equestrian events.

**PanGraf Productions**

360-264-7645

www.pangrafproductions.com

PanGraf Productions has been serving the equine and canine professional community in Washington and Oregon for the past five years.

**Phelps Photography**

Mary Phelps

JJ. Hathaway

www.phelpsphoto.com

Mary and JJ. photograph top shows around the United States and own and operate two premiere equestrian Web sites: www.DressageDaily.com and www.HorsesDaily.com. Mary owns and competes a Classic Shetland driving pony.

**Pics Of You**

434-724-6792

www.picsofyou.com

Pics Of You has been serving the event photography business for over twenty years. Pics Of You specializes in equestrian and motorsports photography. The mobile photography studio offers a wide variety of photographic services, including eventing, equine portraits, dressage, hunter/jumpers, carriage driving, walking/racking, track days, and sport bike racing.

**Jack Schatzberg**

602-522-9777

www.horsephotographer.com

jack@horsephotographer.com

Jack Schatzberg photographed equestrian competitions for more than fifty years. Now retired from the show ring, Schatzberg photographs by appointment at horse farms and ranches throughout the nation. He has a wealth of experience with a great variety of equine breeds, including Miniature Horses. Schatzberg's interest in horse photography was sparked in the 1960s when his daughters learned to ride.

**Alicia Slocumb**

904-803-7363

woodmereshetlands@hughes.net

Alicia Slocumb has been deeply involved with equines for many years. In fact, Slocumb was part of the original committee that formed the division of the Foundation Shetlands. Slocomb, through her farm Woodmere Shetlands, strives to breed Shetland Ponies to have excellent confirmation.

**Stuart Vesty**

www.vestyphoto.com

**Suzanne Sturgill**

Equine Photography by Suzanne

941-753-5414

www.suzannesphoto.com

For two decades, Equine Photography by Suzanne has been meeting and exceeding the needs of the horse community with her exquisite images.

**Washburn Photography**

Terri Washburn

Kenyon, MN

507-789-4657

Terri Washburn and her husband Kirk own Washburn Photography. Terri has been an equine photographer since 1997. She first began photographing Shetlands and Miniature Horses years ago and worked with Jack Schatzberg. After his retirement, Terri's role in small equine photography grew, and now her photographs are seen nationwide.

Special thanks to the following: Matis Associates and Rod and Heather Hart for the photo of the eight-horse-hitch with the Canadian Royal Mounted Police.